REACHING DELINQUENTS
THROUGH READING

Publication Number 313

AMERICAN LECTURE SERIES®

A Monograph in

The BANNERSTONE DIVISION *of*

AMERICAN LECTURES IN PSYCHOLOGY

Edited by

MOLLY HARROWER, Ph. D.

Research and Consulting Psychologist
New York, New York

MELVIN ROMAN, Ph.D.

Formerly, Director of Group Psychotherapy
New York City Court of Domestic Relations

REACHING DELINQUENTS THROUGH READING

CHARLES C THOMAS • PUBLISHER
Springfield • Illinois • U.S.A.

CHARLES C THOMAS · PUBLISHER

BANNERSTONE HOUSE

301-327 East Lawrence Avenue, Springfield, Illinois, U.S.A.

Published simultaneously in the British Commonwealth of Nations by

BLACKWELL SCIENTIFIC PUBLICATIONS, LTD., OXFORD, ENGLAND

Published simultaneously in Canada by

THE RYERSON PRESS, TORONTO

Library of Congress Catalog Card Number: 57-10444

Printed in the United States of America

ACKNOWLEDGMENTS

The investigator welcomes this opportunity to express his indebtedness to Professors Philip Zlatchin, Nila B. Smith and John Tietz, for their helpful suggestions and guidance throughout the course of this study, and to the staff of the Psychiatric Clinic of the Manhattan Children's Court for their support and assistance in the collection of data. He is especially indebted to Dr. Joseph Margolin, Dr. Harris B. Peck and Mr. Carmi Harari for their incisive criticisms of and suggestions toward the therapeutic approach developed in this investigation. And lastly, he owes much to his wife, Harriet, for her continuous encouragement and support.

M. R.

CONTENTS

LIST OF TABLES

Table *Page*

Table   *Page*

LIST OF FIGURES

REACHING DELINQUENTS
THROUGH READING

CHAPTER I

THE PROBLEM

General Statement

IF ONE ADOPTS an organismic frame of reference regarding behavior, it is apparent that one cannot consider the disabilities of an individual apart from his total functioning as an organism. Such a theoretic orientation suggests that we treat the total child. Thus with delinquent children who manifest a reading disability in conjunction with severe emotional disturbance, it seems desirable to integrate therapeutic and remedial efforts. Such an integration will hereafter be referred to as tutorial therapy.

The purpose of this study is to investigate the effectiveness of tutorial group therapy in facilitating psycho-social adjustment and correcting some aspects of reading retardation.

Sub-Problems

1. To what extent does change occur in psycho-social adjustment, and reading ability when tutorial group therapy is administered?

2. To what extent does change occur in psycho-social adjustment and reading ability when group remedial reading is administered?

3. To what extent does change occur in psycho-social adjustment and reading ability when interview group therapy is administered?

Delimitations

This study is limited to the investigation of delinquent

boys on active status in the Treatment Clinic of the Manhattan Children's Court, New York.

The subjects range in age from 13 to 16 years.

All the subjects reveal a reading retardation of 2 or more years and have been found to have reading disabilities.

All the subjects fall within the IQ range of 65 to 95.

All the subjects included in this investigation have exhibited behavior disorders in such a manner as to result in their being adjudged delinquent.

The number of subjects is 21: 7 in each group.

All three treatment groups were conducted by the same therapist, the investigator.

Definition of Terms

For the purpose of this study the following terms will be used as defined below:

Reading Disability is a reading retardation in excess of 2 years below what may be expected of a child's intellectual capacity as indicated by psychological tests.

Group Remedial Reading is a program of reading instruction which is conducted in a group setting and geared to the correction of an individual's disabilities as disclosed by diagnostic indications gained from an oral reading test.

Interview Group Therapy is that form of psychotherapy which is conducted in a group setting and "whose aims and procedures are directed toward improving the mental health of its members" (90, p. 37). In this form of therapy, "results are achieved by virtue of the interaction which takes place among all of the members of the group, including the therapist" (87, p. 157).

Tutorial Group Therapy is that form of psychotherapy which is conducted in a group setting and whose aims and procedures are directed toward the simultaneous correction of reading disabilities and the improvement of mental health. The treatment process consists of the integration of remedial reading and group therapy techniques.

Behavior Disorder refers to the anti social act or acts which led to and precipitated the court appearance of the subjects and resulted in their being adjudged delinquent.

Delinquent as here defined, refers only to the legal status of a child under the statutes of the State of New York.

Psycho-Social Adjustment is defined as the achievement of rapport with the outside world without undue inner tension.

Adjustment is defined as: a) the degree to which inner stability and maturity have been achieved. b) the degree to which rational control in emotional situations is maintained. c) the degree to which rapport is shown with the world outside (25, p. 31).

Basic Assumptions

1. Behavior disorders exist and are analyzable.
2. Reading disabilities exist and are measurable.
3. Psycho-social adjustment is analyzable and to a degree, measurable.

Basic Hypotheses

A prominent characteristic of the delinquent child which the clinical psychologist has shown psychometrically (100), and which can be observed clinically, is his concrete conceptual attitude. "It is true that some delinquents think abstractly, but from personal experience as well as from evidence in the literature, the author believes the delinquent to rely heavily on concrete thought" (108, p. 36).

Clinically, this concrete attitude is manifested in the delinquent's demand to be "shown" by the therapist that he is not being punished and will be helped. He asks for real, meaningful goals rather than being satisfied with the more abstract idea that the therapist wants to help him and that "talking" will help. Thus, it appears necessary to anchor therapy in an area where the delinquent child is aware of, or can be made aware of, his inadequacy and can "see," in concrete terms, the possibility of help. The advantages of a therapeutic approach which focuses on and grows out of the reading disability seem to be that the delinquent is aware of the problem, desirous of help, and that his conscious willingness to cooperate can be elicited.

It has been shown (33) that meeting the emotional needs of children who have a reading disability is an important factor in correcting the retardation. It has also been indicated (10, p. 152) that specific remedial help for disturbed children tends to strengthen their egos and facilitate psychosocial adjustment.

In view of the above, the following hypotheses are under consideration:

1. That tutorial group therapy will improve psychosocial adjustment, and 1a) that the tutorial group therapy subjects (experimental group) will show greater improvement in adjustment than the members in either of the other two groups, i.e., remedial reading or interview group.

2. That tutorial group therapy will result in the improvement of reading ability, and 2a) that the tutorial group therapy subjects will show greater improvement in reading than the members in either of the two control groups.

The Need for the Study

The need for this study stems from certain critical social realities which workers in the field of delinquency are coming to recognize as of primary importance. In retracing the course of the development of an individual's delinquent behavior, it is not unusual to find the triad: reading retardation . . . truancy . . . delinquency. This is not to suggest that failure in reading is the basic causative factor in such cases. Many children with reading disabilities are not and never become delinquents, but many delinquents first manifest their difficulties in the development of reading disabilities.

That reading is of vital importance in the total life adjustment of every child, is indicated by the role that is assigned to this subject in the elementary school, the variety of instructional techniques that have originated in relation to it, and the large number of studies that have been conducted in this area. Authorities (89) agree that academic achievement in most school subjects is directly related to one's reading ability. Unfortunately, many children fail to develop adequate reading skills.

To this point Gates states:

Despite the quantity of experimental data, the wealth of ingenious teaching devices, the range of interesting children's reading material, and the large amount of school time available for teaching reading, a surprisingly large number of school children still experience difficulty in acquiring satisfactory reading skills (45, p. 2).

A recent survey by Traxler (122) indicates that approximately 10% of the school population of America requires special aid because of retardation in reading. A survey conducted by the writer at the Manhattan Children's Court revealed that 84% of cases carried by the Treatment Clinic present the problem of reading retardation in conjunction with personality disorders and antisocial behavior.

Fabian (34) in a comparative study of the incidence of reading disability in several clinical settings revealed the following: an incidence of 10% in a school sample; 33% in a child guidance clinic sample; 62% in a sample from a child placement agency; 73% in the population of a psychiatric hospital's children's ward, and 83% in a sample of pre-delinquent and delinquent children.

The above-mentioned surveys clearly indicate the magnitude of the problem and highlight its significance to Children's Courts throughout the country.

A variety of approaches are utilized in attempting to correct reading retardation. The techniques used are usually related to the therapists' or teachers' beliefs concerning the causes of the disability and the function of the setting in which the treatment takes place. Traxler surveying current procedures in remedial teaching reports: "The replies to the questionnaire show that many different approaches to instruction in remedial reading are used. The questionnaire listed thirteen kinds of reading procedures, and all of these were checked by sizeable proportions of the respondents. In addition, nearly fifty other teaching procedures were listed" (122, p. 121). A review of recent literature in the field of remedial reading reveals a trend away from formal tutorial techniques and an emphasis on therapeutically oriented programs. This trend stems from the understanding that a reading disability, although specific in one sense, is really an organismic problem. Effective treatment must deal with the total personality of the individual rather than with some particular set of intellectual or sensory factors.

> Corrective measures should not be limited to the area of deficiency, but should be applied to the larger issues and the psychological dynamics underlying this deficiency. The teacher cannot ignore the faculty values of the child, his mistaken self concepts and erroneous approaches. Efforts to change them should become the essence of remedial teaching. Individual, and particularly group discussions, can successfully influence children in changing their values and concepts (30, p. 3).

The growing acceptance of group therapy and the increased frequency with which it is being used as a treatment technique for psychological disorders, educational disabilities and social maladjustments makes it imperative that we continue to clarify its nature and scope, and evaluate its results. Research oriented toward the development of new techniques with a constant orientation toward careful evaluation, will assure growth in a significant field. The study under consideration is oriented toward the evaluation of a new form of group therapy in order to determine how we might best meet the specific individualized needs of certain delinquent children. In discussing the question of differential therapy, Slavson states:

> Differential therapy and individualization increase the pertinence of the treatment plan and enhance its effectiveness and efficiency. The more appropriately the tools of any craft are employed, the more is effectiveness assured. As the therapist is able to fit the method of treatment to the particular patient, the more likely is he to obtain desirable results (113, p. 293).

The specific significance of the study under consideration is reflected in a recent statement by the Children's Bureau:

> In view of the large amount of time, money and energy invested in a variety of treatment programs for delinquent children, and the conflicting claims made for specific measures, it is particularly important that research be directed toward the identification of differential methods of treatment of juvenile delinquents and the development of criteria for evaluating their effects (134, p. 4).

CHAPTER II

RELATED LITERATURE

Introduction

READING is of fundamental importance in the academic life of children and is in many ways related to one's total life adjustment. From the earliest times to the present, American educators have made reading the core of the educative process. Smith reports that "reading was the most important subject in our early American schools, and it has continued to be the most important subject all through the years of our national growth (117, p. iii). The scope and volume of research that has been conducted in this area is illustrated by an index (12) issued in 1945 which lists 8,278 references. Some of the areas in which research has been conducted are: reading readiness and beginning reading; reading interests and attitudes; reading and its relationship to other school subjects; reading tests, remedial methods, and many other related problems.

In recent years, a great deal of attention has been given to the relationship between psycho-social adjustment and the reading process. Many studies, some of which are described in this chapter, attempted to ascertain the specific psychological and/or sociological bases for reading difficulties. In this regard, some investigators have hypothecated that correcting social and/or emotional problems will remedy reading retardation. Others have suggested that specific remedial help for disturbed children tends to facilitate psycho-social adjustment. Thus, there is currently much controversy with regard to the question: remedial reading and/ or psycho-therapy? It is with this question that the present study is primarily concerned.

The Etiology of Reading Disability

Reading disability, so ubiquitous a symptom of childhood, has attracted specialists from many fields of research including several branches of education, psychology and medicine. Divergent opinions, on several aspects of the problem have arisen out of these multidisciplinary approaches. The many theories on etiology that have been presented in the past 75 years of investigation of reading retardation have been classified by Fabian (34) under the following four headings: 1) organ centered; 2) school centered; 3) child centered, and 4) family centered.

Organ Centered

The peripheral and central organs of perception—visual, auditory and kinesthetic—were the first to be examined in connection with the development of reading disability. Javal (60) in 1879 first called attention to the occurrence of faulty eye movements in retarded readers. Ocular pathology resulting in myopia, aneisokonia and other visual defects has been causally related to reading difficulties by ophthalmologists (31). Interestingly, an opthalmologist, Hinshelwood (57), challenged the theory which gives importance to peripheral eye defects and suggested instead that central brain damage, or developmental brain abnormalities accounted for reading disturbance.

In 1925 Orton (84) repudiated Hinshelwood's theory that word-blindness is based on focal agenesis and presented the hypothesis that in reading disability we deal with a physiological variant. Orton (85) felt that faulty unilateral cerebral dominance causes images formed in one side of the brain to conflict with those formed in the other side. This conflict of images subsequently results, he claims, in the child's experiencing great difficulty in learning to read.

The present status of Orton's theory is still that of an unproved hypothesis. While it has met with fairly wide acceptance among neurologists, its basic neurological assumptions have been challenged by studies of the effects of brain operations upon lateral dominance (116).

Another major neurological theory is that of Dearborn (27) who, like Orton, believes that reading disabilities stem from a confusion of lateral dominance. Dearborn, however, places major responsibility on confusion in motor activity, while Orton's theory stresses confusion in mental imagery.

School Centered

To the school teacher reading retardation is not a theoretical issue. Confronted with the problem of coping with a condition that generally affects 10 to 15% of the school population (122) educators have searched for enlightenment and help. They welcomed the organ centered theories but found them inadequate in every day application. Organic defects, whether of the ears, eyes or brain, can produce learning difficulties. But, the average school child is no more damaged organically than he is mentally defective, as was the impression before intelligence tests came into use in schools. Children with serious visual defects often learn to read without difficulty and dominance problems are as common in good readers as in poor readers (132).

During the early years of research in the area of reading disability, and continuing to the present, many investigators have tried to resolve the problem by attempting to improve instructional methods and procedures. Smith has stated:

More innovations have been effected in reading instruction in the first thirty years of the present century than

during the entire three hundred years of American history
antedating that period (117, p. 246).

Despite the marked improvement in teaching methods
many children still cannot learn to read. Recognizing this,
educators have been reluctant to attribute reading retardation solely to inadequate teaching programs. Gates (43)
in his early writings, mentioned the possibility that personality disturbances might contribute to the development of
reading disability, and has more recently given increasing
attention to these factors. Similarly, educators have come
to recognize many children whose personal problems and
not the teaching methods interfered with their ability to
learn.

Child Centered

During the 1920's a number of writers concerned themselves with the relationship between personality factors and
learning difficulties: Jones (61) reported that subject disabilities were often due to an inhibition of interest because
the subject-content was unconsciously associated with some
personally unpleasant idea or topic. Meek (74) observed
that children showed marked individual differences in their
emotional attitudes toward learning to read and Hincks
(56) published a series of case studies in which she emphasized the relationship between emotional maladjustment
and reading disability. Monroe (76) reported that emotional problems can be observed in almost every case of
reading disability and that these problems ranged from
severe and persistent to mild and easily overcome. She
stated that faulty attitudes toward reading generally disap-
pear when the child learns to read. She noted several types
of reactions to reading disability: withdrawal, apathy, hostility and resistance.

Following these early studies, a large group of investigators reported on the personality of the retarded reader.

These reports were essentially descriptive and non-interpretive. Hardwick (50) for example, states that children with reading disabilities are timid and manifest feelings of inferiority. Bennett (9) in describing retarded readers notes fears, loneliness, inattentiveness, lack of persistence and a tendency to withdraw from social relations. Gates (43) points out that children with reading problems are withdrawn, prone to daydreaming, overly sensitive and lack the aggressiveness necessary for effective adaptation to the learning situation. Tulchin (123) suggests that undesirable patterns of behavior and personality maladjustment can often be traced to reading disability. Witty and Kopel (132) state that 50% of their population of retarded readers are burdened by fears and anxieties which require a program of reeducation geared toward the re-establishment of selfconfidence and security.

Gann, on the basis of an intensive study of the personality of the retarded reader, concludes that:

> . . . the findings in this study may be applied to the practical school situation where the retarded reader should be considered as a personality problem, as well as a learning problem. Consideration of his reading difficulty cannot be made apart from his personality adjustment and his attitudes toward the reading experience (40, p. 22).

Siegel (111), in a recent study, compared the personality structures of 42 known cases of reading disability with the personality structures of 42 subjects who presented other clinical problems. On the basis of this study he reports that "the poor readers were actually a clinical population characterized by neurotic anxiety and internalized conflict. No single personality pattern was characteristic of the Reading Group, which showed a range of disturbance such as might be found in any group of emotionally disturbed children" (111, p. 2).

In a similar view, Hirsch claims that there are "hundreds of youngsters who have language difficulty and who suffer from a psychological disturbance as well, children who need help in both areas" (58, p. 196). The current general acceptance of the relationship between personality factor and reading disability is indicated by Russell in The Yearbook of the National Society for the Study of Education:

> Reading abilities and personality adjustments are closely related. Teachers have known for years that the child with reading disabilities often has personality difficulties. Summaries of the research in the field indicate that personality maladjustments do not always lead to reading difficulties, but they are often causes, concomitants or results of such difficulties (104, p. 27).

This seems to be especially relevant to delinquent children who as a group manifest a significantly high incidence of reading retardation in conjunction with psycho-social disturbance.

What is the relationship between psychopathology and learning disability? For many years, psychoanalytic investigators have been concerned with this question. There is a growing literature contributed by them on the subject of the influence of psychodynamic processes in reading disability. The dynamic considerations range from diffuse blocks in children with infantile, pleasure-driven personalities who cannot accept the frustration that accompanies learning, to specific inhibitions stemming from threatening fantasies.

Weisskopf (127) in a recent article states that learning is a process in which children, because of the need for the rewards of parental approval and love, "put on the tight corset of cultural demands." He indicates that learning disability is an overdetermined symptom which may stem from a variety of causes. For example, a child may unconsciously prevent himself from learning in order to punish overbearing parents. In another situation, reading disability may reflect an unconscious need for self-punishment. In describing various neurotic processes which affect learning Weisskopf suggests that inhibitions which occur from specific threatening aspects of cognition may be displaced onto the process of intellection. Thus, a learning disturbance may result from inhibition based on guilt feelings stemming from the child's early sexual curiosity. A variety of psychological threats are described which may cause the child to avoid intellection. The child feels, "what I don't know, won't hurt me" and uses ignorance as a defensive facade.

Mahler (70) suggests that reading disability may be the protest of an infantile child against growth, or be the outcome in a phobic child who invests the learning situation with excessive anxiety. Strachey (120) has indicated that in some children learning takes on "oral" and/or "anal" significance and becomes enmeshed in the conflicts active at these pre-genitally fixated levels. In a similar view, Klein (63) indicates that for those children whose neurotic conflicts are largely concerned with the repression of aggressive impulses, sublimated expression in reading may not be permissible to ego and super-ego.

Blanchard (20), in her psychoanalytic contribution to the problem of reading disabilities states that they are the results of severe limitations in instinctual drives and closely related to early peeping activities. Reversals, according to Blanchard, represent the symbolic expression of hostility and aggression and reading content is associated directly and symbolically with unconscious emotional conflicts. Blanchard (20) differentiates two types of reading disability cases: 1) the non-neurotic who develops emotional conflict largely out of an inability to learn to read, and 2) the neurotic whose reading disability is a symptom of and stems from his emotional conflicts. She states:

> A common etiological factor was a difficulty in handling aggression, with excessive guilt and anxiety over hostile, destructive or sadistic impulses and fantasies, which frequently were oral in form. The neurotic symptom (reading disability) originates from an effort to solve ambivalent guilt conflicts, a disguised expression for repressed instinctual drives, but at the same time relieves anxiety and guilt about these drives through the self punishment of illness and also satisfies the guilty need for punishment by exposing the child to a situation of failure at school and criticism both there and at home (20, p. 70).

More recently Sylvester and Kunst (121) indicated that a child's earliest interpersonal experiences may predispose him to poor reading. They stated that the learning process may be wrought with anxiety generated by the child's destructive impulses toward persons on whom he depends.

In summarizing the variety of views on the relationship between emotional disturbance and reading disability, Robinson states that, "it seems evident that emotional difficulties may cause reading disability in the beginning and that this disability may, in turn, result in frustration, which further blocks learning and again intensifies the frustration" (99, p. 78).

Family Centered

It may be stated, and with justification, that familial considerations rightfully belong in the discussion of theories which are child centered. It is being introduced separately in order to add another dimension in the understanding of the forces which shape the psychological reactions of the child. Fabian has pointed out that:

> ... The child brings his family to school. Society, through the teacher, is then given its first opportunity to take inventory of the family's work. The way in which the child relates to his classmates, teachers and other adults in the

school, his ability to adjust to new situations, to compete and to master, these reactions, attitudes, prejudices, and habits are patterns that have already been laid down prior to his school enrollment. The way in which the child learns has already been established (34, p. 6).

Parent attitudes and backgrounds in relation to reading failure are treated by Preston. She states that, "evidently neither wealth, intelligence, or education, singly or together presupposes an atmosphere fit for the upbringing of children" (92, p. 173). She further indicates that it is unjust to place total blame for reading failure on the child and one must assess the influence of the home setting. Robinson reports that, "maladjusted homes or poor intra-family relationships were found to be contributing causes in fifty-four and one-half per cent of the cases studied." Fabian emphasizes this finding in a recent report which states:

> ... The striking clinical feature, evolving from the present study in which comparative studies of several clinical settings were made, is the high incidence of reading disability, usually of a severe order, in children who are heavily burdened with familiar psychopathology (34, p. 9).

Cunningham (24) describes an unusual situation which arose in a mill town during the war when the mothers were pressed into factory work. Their 5 year olds, who could not be accommodated in the kindergarten, were admitted directly into the first grade. An unusually high incidence of reading disability developed in these children as they advanced to the upper grades. Fabian in reviewing this report states:

> The symptom of reading disability was, in this unplanned community experiment, an epidemological index comparable to the wave of enuresis which engulfed the British children who were evacuated to the countryside during the war and to the symptom, miner's nystagmus, arising

out of social and economic dislocations, which Halliday studied. The factor of inadequate reading readiness was no doubt aggravated by disruption of familial units caused by the mass exodus of the mothers during an important developmental period in the lives of their children (34, p. 11).

The significance of familial psychopathology and the environmental forces which engender it seem particularly relevant to the understanding of the reading disability in a delinquent child. In a recent paper, Roman, Margolin and Harari state:

> Our case studies indicate that many delinquent children enter school with a characteristic lack of learning readiness and an equally characteristic readiness to discharge hostility when frustrated. The school by virtue of content and process confronts the low socio-economic child with a new set of frustrating experiences which in some ways realistically confirm his already distorted picture of authority and precipitates the development of the reading disability . . . truancy . . . delinquency syndrome (102, p. 5).

It seems clear that the child brings to school not only his family, but also the environment in which he and his family live and learn. Thus in their paper, the same authors conclude that:

> . . . in the majority of our cases conflict between the middle class educational experience and lower socio-economic class forces induces certain psychodynamic processes which tend to produce reading retardation and emotional disturbance (102, p. 11).

Remedial Reading and/or Psychotherapy

Zirbes, Newell and Hardwick were some of the first investigators who dealt with the problem of correcting reading difficulties. Zirbes (133 in a case study investigation of 28 subjects with reading disabilities found that the reading difficulties were so closely related to personality problems that the latter must be considered in planning remedial procedures.

In similar fashion, Newell (82) suggested that the first problem in treating a child with reading difficulties is to correct the emotional attitudes associated with the disability. She indicated that there was emotional tension in every situation requiring remedial work, and added that failure to read on the part of intelligent children caused misunderstanding and anxiety.

Hardwick (50) stresses the need for accurate diagnosis in terms of choosing the most appropriate treatment approach. It is her position that if the personality problem is basic to the reading disability, the emotional difficulties must be treated before we can bring about any improvement in reading. If, however, the emotional problems are secondary and stem from the reading disability, she states that the emotional problems cannot be resolved until we first correct the reading disability.

Damereau (25) on the other hand, found that removal of the disability did not seem to improve behavior. She hypothesized that if reading disability were a cause of emotional maladjustment, then treatment resulting in improvement of reading ability would result in improved interpersonal relations. On the basis of her study she concluded that improvement in reading bears little relationship to improvement in behavior.

From the point of view of the classroom teacher, Addy (2) suggested that there should be lessened emphasis on instructional techniques and greater consideration of the adjustment of the child to himself and the environment. He indicates that the child's social, intellectual, emotional and physical development are related to his behavior in the classroom and that disturbance in any developmental area may interfere with his ability to learn to read.

Gunzberg (48) like Addy, believes that the teaching of reading involves offering emotional support to the unstable and insecure. He indicates that research into the relationship between the child's social and emotional adjustment and his attitude toward reading is the most promising approach to the problem of the unsuccessful reader. Pearson in a recent article states that:

> In recent years psychologists and educators tend to regard the majority, if not all, of the children who seem to have difficulty in learning their school work as suffering from neurotic problems and to refer them to child psychiatrists and child psychoanalysts (86, p. 448).

Accepting the assumption that remedial work cannot be approached mechanically, a number of investigators began to focus on the individual and his feelings, and studies emerged concerning the effectiveness of psychotherapy in the correction of reading retardation. Axline, reporting on one such study states:

> This study indicates that a non-directive approach might be helpful in solving certain "reading problems." It indicates that it would be worthwhile to set up research projects to test this hypothesis further: That non-directive therapeutic procedures applied to children with reading problems are effective not only in bringing about a better personal adjustment, but also in building up a readiness to read (5, p. 69).

Redmount (98) investigated the relationship between improvement in emotional adjustment and improvement in reading. The results of his 6 weeks "pre" and "post" study are that: reading tests indicate 48% with higher scores and 12% with lower scores; Rorschach tests revealed that 39% made positive gains in adjustment and 26% showed a loss in adjustment.

Bills, working with a class of third grade slow learners

concludes that:

1. Significant changes in reading ability occurred as a result of the play therapy experience.
2. Personal changes may occur in non-directive play therapy in as little as six individual and three group play therapy sessions, and
3. There appears to be no common personality maladjustment present in this group of retarded readers (13, p. 148).

Another example of the psychotherapeutic approach in the correction of reading disabilities is the dramatic dialogue technique developed at the Harvard Graduate School of Education. McGann (72) describes this technique as one involving two characters in an unbroken conversational situation, with content determined by the needs and interests of the readers. Thus, the dialogue serves as a vehicle for emotional release. McGann indicates that this technique satisfies the emotional needs of retarded readers and facilitates rapport and motivation.

Fisher (36) studied the effectiveness of group therapy as a means of correcting reading retardation. The subjects were 30 residents of the Children's Village who were divided into three groups and equated for reading achievement and intelligence. One group received only remedial reading, another received only group therapy and still another received group therapy in addition to their remedial instruction. The results of his study indicate that his "pure" therapy group made greater improvement in reading than his non-therapy group, although the group that received therapy and remedial reading did not show significantly greater improvement in reading than the non-therapy group. It was concluded that meeting the emotional needs of children who have a disability is an important factor in the correction of reading retardation. Fisher in discussing his results suggests that in the group that received psychotherapy and remedial reading the negative attitudes toward remedial reading and the remedial teacher, which were not dealt with therapeutically, impeded their therapeutic progress.

On the basis of Fisher's study one might argue that it is as unrealistic for a therapist to ignore the reading problems of his patient as it is for the teacher to ignore the emotional problems of her student.

Dreikurs in a recent article states:

Corrective measures should not be limited to the area of deficiency, but should be applied to the larger issues and the psychological dynamics underlying this deficiency. The teacher cannot ignore the faulty values of the child, his mistaken self concepts and erroneous approaches. Efforts to change them should become the essence of remedial teaching. Individual, and particularly group discussions, can successfully influence children in changing their values and concepts (30, p. 4).

Despite the variety of evidence indicating the effectiveness of psychotherapy in the correcting of reading retardation, the significance of the various approaches to the treatment of delinquents has not been established. In a chapter titled "The Clinical Dilemma," Redl and Wineman conclude that delinquent children are "beyond the reach of education and below the grip of the psychiatric interview" (96, p. 240). They elaborate this conclusion by pointing out that:

. . . good education is not enough for the cure of children who hate. Rather, the reverse comes closer to the truth: in order for a good educational diet to take hold of these children at all, their basic ego disturbances must be repaired first (96, p. 242).

. . . once you take children as severely disturbed as we described the children who hate to be, the "psychiatric interview technique" does not offer enough of a strategic change. Rather the reverse is true: in order for "psychiatric interview techniques" of any style even to be usable on them, their ego first needs a considerable degree of repair in the areas where it cannot perform . . . It seems that there is no way out of the dilemma but the invention of a new design, which offers us opportunities of strategy in a different dimension than either good education or thorough psychiatric treatment in themselves seem to grant (96, p. 245).

Assuming that Redl's position was essentially correct, Roman, Margolin and Harari, in a recent paper deal with the reading problems of delinquent children state:

. . . it was our conviction that we could not consider the reading problem of the delinquent child apart from his total functioning as an individual. Effective treatment, as we saw it, involved a modified psychotherapeutic approach incorporating treatment techniques designed to deal with the child's unproductive attitudes and emotional conflicts and remedial techniques designed to yield those positive educational experiences leading to a more satisfactory orientation toward reading, school and other areas of maladjustment (102, p. 12).

The need for additional research is thus pointed up along the lines of the present study.

CHAPTER III

PROCEDURE IN COLLECTING DATA

The Setting

THIS STUDY was conducted at the Treatment Clinic of the New York City Children's Court under the auspices of the Bureau of Mental Health Services and the privately financed Court Intake Project. The Psychiatric Clinic (recently renamed Bureau of Mental Health Services) is housed in the court building and was originally established as a diagnostic center in 1916. In 1937 the Treatment Clinic was added as a special resource. The Diagnostic and Treatment Clinics remained, however, two distinct entities separated legally. The Treatment Clinic was financed by private funds up until 1946, at which time the City assumed major financial responsibility for its operation.

All children referred to the Treatment Clinic have been adjudicated neglected or delinquent, and are placed on probation. The clinic population ranges in age from 7 to 16. During the period of treatment at the clinic, the role of the Probation Officer is taken over by the Clinic Therapist, and thus, the child remains on probation to the Court until the time of discharge from treatment.

In 1947, 10 years after the Treatment Clinic had been organized, the first attempts in group therapy were made using interview group therapy, i.e., discussions. The first groups were composed of children who had been treated without success in individual psychotherapy. The groups were organized on an experimental basis with the expressed hope that they might benefit those children who were found inaccessible in individual treatment.

In the past 7 years the Clinic has conducted many therapy groups for both children and parents. At present groups are being used for diagnostic as well as therapeutic purposes.

Subjects

Each subject used in this study has met the criteria outlined in Delimitations. The population therefore consisted of 21 male subjects between the ages of 13 and 16, whose achievement in reading was at least 2 years below expectancy for their mental ability and chronological age, and whose IQ's ranged between 65 to 95. All had been adjudged delinquent and were on active status with the Treatment Clinic of Manhattan Children's Court.

For the purpose of disguisement and case identification, the subjects will be designated by the number of the experimental group to which they were assigned and by a code letter arbitrarily given to each member.

The 21 subjects were divided into three groups as follows:

RG I —to receive group remedial reading (7 subjects)

RG II —to receive tutorial group therapy (7 subjects)

RG III—to receive interview group therapy (7 subjects)

The groups were matched by a paired comparison method.

Methodology

In order to test the stated hypothesis that tutorial group therapy will be more effective than either group remedial reading or interview group therapy in facilitating psychosocial adjustment and correcting some aspects of reading retardation, the following procedures were employed. The subjects were divided into three groups selected on the basis of matched samples so that they would be equated for age, intelligence and reading grade. Group I received a program of remedial reading in a group setting. Group II received a program of tutorial group therapy. Group III received a program of interview group therapy. In order to control the variable of the therapist's personality, all three treatment groups were conducted by the same therapist. This had the virtue of providing constancy of therapist's personality but rested upon another assumption, i.e., that the therapist would be equally skillful, perceptive and objective in each of the three procedures.

Materials Used

The following techniques were used in evaluating each subject ("before" and "after" treatment).

Case Histories

A detailed case history of each subject was obtained by a psychiatric social worker. This included pertinent data regarding the subject's early development, school and family history, health, socio-economic status, siblings, interests, etc. The case history was supplemented by a description of subject's behavior and personality adjustment as reflected during an interview prior to initiation of the treatment program.

Intelligence Test

An abbreviated form of the Wechsler Intelligence Scale for Children (126) (hereafter referred to as the WISC) was employed as a measure of intelligence. This downward extension of the Wechsler Bellevue Intelligence Scales is standardized for children aged 5 to 16 years. The abbreviated form of the WISC which was used in this study consists of the following three subtests: Comprehension; Arithmetic, and Similarities (hereafter referred to as the CAS). The abbreviated form was used in this study simply because this is the routine procedure by which children are assessed in the Psychiatric Clinic of the Manhattan Children's Court. The time limitations of the clinical setting in which this study was conducted precluded the utilization of the full form of the WISC.

The history of short forms of the Wechsler Bellevue Intelligence Scale is replete with published research. Hunt (59), using 528 "normal" Naval recruits, reported a correlation of .91 between the CAS and full scale Wechsler Bellevue IQ's. Rabin (93), in a study of 200 state hospital patients, ages 15 to 36, reports a correlation of .956 between the CAS and the full Wechsler Bellevue IQ's. Springer (119), in a study of 100 Naval recruits suspected of retardation, indicates a correlation of .92 between the CAS and full scale Wechsler Bellevue.

No studies were found to cause the investigator to raise serious questions about the validity of the shorter form of the WISC employed in this experiment. And, since the common variance (R^2) between full and brief form was as great as 80 to 90%, the short form was accepted as an adequate measure of intelligence for the purposes of this study.

In accordance with the above, the CAS of the WISC was employed in this study, and was administered, scored and interpreted according to the manual provided for this test (126).

Reading Test

In judging the reading ability of each child, only two aspects of the reading process were examined, rate of oral reading and ability to recognize printed words. The Gray's Oral Reading Paragraphs (47) test was used. This test contains 12 paragraphs of increasing difficulty, ranging from first grade to secondary school level. Every error made is recorded for later analysis and each paragraph is timed. The number of pronunciation errors and rate of oral reading are combined to get a grade score. The Gray Standardized Oral Reading Paragraphs test is a recognized and statistically validated measure of oral reading ability which has been "used as a regular part of the Monroe battery, as well as independently" (50, p. 185). This test was chosen because of its routine use in the psychological battery administered to children at Children's Court Clinic and in many other clinics and reading centers.

The investigator recognizes that one of the deficiencies of the above mentioned test is in its omission of a measure of reading comprehension. The specific nature of the reading ability measured by this test might be best described as recognition of words in oral reading.

Projective Techniques

The use of projective techniques in the evaluation of personality has been well established in the literature (105). The essential feature of a projective technique has been described by Frank as, ". . . it evokes from the subject what is in various ways, expressive of his private world and personality process" (39, p. 47).

The experiences of clinicians in the field of remedial reading indicate that the questionnaire type of personality test is often unreliable with reading disability since there is a limited or questionable comprehension of verbal material and fails to avoid the weakness of being open to conscious manipulation even when content and wording are thoroughly understood. In view of the above, the following projective techniques were used:

Rorschach

This test is generally regarded as the most widely used tool in diagnostic personality testing (94).

Reliability (38) and validity (8) studies have been conducted supporting the value of the instrument and over

800 bibliographic references are available which deal with this test. The Rorschach test was therefore used in this study as the primary tool for the evaluation of personality.

Figure Drawings

The Human Figure Drawing Test was given to each subject. This is a relatively recent tool in personality investigation. The interpretation of the drawings is qualitative and subjective and is based upon clinical experience. The drawings are usually used as an adjunct to the Rorschach to aid in the personality study. The drawings were used toward this end in this investigation. Machover (69) presents a beginning approach toward systematization of drawing analyses. The drawings obtained in this study were interpreted along the lines suggested by her.

Szondi

In general, the Szondi Test (29) fulfills two of the major requirements for a projective technique. First, it purports to reveal the private world of the individual selecting the pictures. It attempts to reveal the dynamics of his basic needs and drives. Secondly, the subject is not conscious of the fact that he is doing just that. He is not aware of the interpretations that may be placed on his test performance.

The ease of administration and the lack of need for verbal response on the part of the subject recommend the use of this technique with the population represented in this investigation. The Szondi Test seems particularly useful with linguistically handicapped individuals.

Thus far, there are no crucial experiments that would validate this test. The present "evidence" is of the nature of empirical proof (28). The validation is clinical validation by those who employ the method (52).

As indicated above the Rorschach, Figure Drawing and Szondi Tests were administered to each subject. Neither the

Figure Drawing nor the Szondi Test was interpreted independently. Each was used as an adjunct to the Rorschach in terms of assessing each subject in several areas of psychological functioning. Each test makes a unique contribution to the delineation of personality features and psychopathology of the total personality. Each is a standardized situation designed to elicit clear and instructive instances of the subject's style of thinking, which, in turn, throws light on dominant trends of his global personality organization. The contribution of each test is, however, richest when amplified, qualified or re-emphasied by the results of the other tests, for the tests are fundamentally congruent with each other and merely approach the individual from different vantage points.

Testing Conditions

All the testing was done at the Psychiatric Clinic of the Manhattan Children's Court by the investigator and two other qualified psychologists who are trained beyond the Master's degree and have more than 3 years of clinical experience. Each subject was tested individually.

Adjustment Ratings

Adjustment signs or ratings were used in the present study as an adjunct to clinical evaluation, as a check on clinical observation, and as a measure of the effectiveness of treatment. It should be noted that the use of adjustment signs or ratings in the attempt to identify disturbed persons, to predict academic success, and to differentiate clinical groups has had considerable success (75, 78). To evaluate the changes in adjustment the following techniques were used:

Davidson Rorschach Signs

Davidson (26) has constructed a list of 17 signs which can be obtained easily and objectively from a Rorschach record and used as a measure of adjustment. Evidence concerning the internal consistency of this list of signs is offered by Davidson in her review (26) of the published and unpublished studies on this set of signs. It is shown that this list does differentiate among individuals and between groups. The limited range of the means and standard deviations obtained from varied groups are offered as evidence for its general applicability.

In this investigation, the Rorschach protocols of each subject were assessed by this technique and given an adjustment rating.

Haggerty-Olson-Wickman Behavior Rating Scale Schedule B

The Behavior Rating Scale, Schedule B (hereafter referred to as H.O.W.) (49), consists of a graphic rating scale for each of 35 intellectual, physical, social and emotional traits. By use of the Behavior Rating Scale the behavior status of a problem child may be designated in quantitative terms on the basis of his relative position on a distribution of problem tendencies in the general school population. Validity (83) and reliability (83) studies have been conducted supporting the value of this technique.

Schedule B of the Behavior Rating Scale seems particularly suited for use in a "before" and "after" study of behavioral changes effected by treatment. The scale allows for five adjustment ratings: intellectual; physical; social; emotional, and total.

Each subject was rated on the basis of his group behavior in the initial five sessions and in the last five sessions. The ratings were made by a fully trained psychologist who functioned as observer in all three groups.

Group Observations

A specially trained psychologist functioned as an observer in all three groups in order to record from direct observation of group meetings, the verbal and non-verbal communications exchanged, the interrelationship of significant events, and the changes that occurred from meeting to meeting.

Steps and Organization in Collecting Data

It is assumed that the process of selection for referral to the Psychiatric Clinic of Manhattan Children's Court has tended to create a relatively homogeneous population. The group may be broadly described as delinquent, non-psychotic, from a low socio-economic environment, in good physical condition, and of educable intelligence. The technique for establishing the three experimental groups described above in Methodology is based upon the information contained in Lindquist (67), and is detailed below.

The 21 subjects used in this study were divided into three equated groups containing seven in each group. The groups were matched in the following manner: The subjects were listed in ascending rank order by chronological age and then divided into three groups, the youngest seven boys, the middle seven boys and the oldest seven boys. Each group was then ranked in ascending order for each of the following factors: reading grade and IQ. Each subject then had two ranks. The numerical rank for the two factors was totaled for each subject in order to obtain a score which was then used to create the matched groups. For example, in ranking the youngest seven boys the following procedure was used: (The lowest numerical rank indicates the lowest ability.)

Subject	Chronological Age	Reading Grade Rank	IQ Rank	Total Score
A.	13-0	3	5	8
B.	13-4	2	7	9

After a total score had been obtained for each subject in each of the age groups, the subjects were then listed in ascending rank order on the basis of the total scores within each age group. The youngest seven were the first seven in the ranking and the oldest seven were the last seven, as described above.

The three groups were then constructed by alternating the order of assignment to a group in the following manner:

Group				Rank			
I	1	6	8	11	15	16	19
II	2	4	9	10	14	18	20
III	3	5	7	12	13	17	21

This was arrived at by listing the six possible combinations of I II III (III II I, II I III, etc.) on separate pieces of paper and then drawing for each placement. Thus, the first drawing was I II III, the second drawing II III I, third III I II, etc. Assigning the subjects to groups in the manner described above tended to randomize the process of selection so that the three groups were equated.

The extent to which the three experimental groups were matched can be seen in Table I which presents the mean scores for each of the three groups with regard to Intelligence Quotient and Reading Grade before the period of treatment.

TABLE I

COMPARISON OF "PRE" IQ AND READING GRADE MEANS

Experimental Group	Mean IQ	Mean Reading Grade
RG I	79.7	2.8
RG II	81.0	2.4
RG III	77.6	2.8

Tables II and III contain the results of the analysis of variance of the above indicated group means. As can be seen from the data below (Tables II and III), the mean differences were not significant.

TABLE II

SUMMARY OF ANALYSIS OF VARIANCE ON "PRE" IQ MEANS

Source	Sum of Squares	df	Mean Square	F
Between groups	41.9	2	20.95	N.S.
Within groups	991.2	18	55.06	

TABLE III
SUMMARY OF ANALYSIS OF VARIANCE ON "PRE" READING GRADE MEANS

Source	Sum of Squares	df	Mean Square	F
Between groups	.6	2	.30	N.S.
Within groups	44.9	18	2.49	

As a further check on the equating of groups, this time with regard to psycho-social factors, the "pre" treatment data on the Haggerty-Olson-Wickman Behavior Rating Scale were analyzed. The results of this matching check appear in Table IV.

TABLE IV
SUMMARY OF ANALYSIS OF VARIANCE ON "PRE" H.O.W. TOTAL MEANS

Source	Sum of Squares	df	Mean Square	F
Between groups	1080.66	2	540.33	N.S.
Within Groups	1023.80	6	170.63	N.S.
Residual	7417.35	12	618.11	
Total	9521.81	20		

Table IV indicates that there were no significant mean differences between the groups on the H.O.W. Behavior Rating Scale Total score. Thus, it is evident that the three experimental groups were equated in regard to intelligence, reading grade and ratings of psycho-social behavior.

At the beginning and at the end of the investigation all the subjects were assessed by the techniques described above in Materials Used.

The subjects met with their respective groups for one and one-half hour sessions once a week for a period of 7 months. All of the group meetings were observed by a trained psychologist.

The Remedial Reading Group (hereafter referred to as RGI) subjects were told that they had been referred to the Clinic by their Probation Officers because of their reading difficulties. They were told that they can learn to read if they "try" and that the therapist has been successful in teaching other children with similar problems.

The remedial work with the group followed the principles and procedures described by Harris (51). In general, instruction was provided in such aspects of reading as the development of basic sight vocabulary, word analysis techniques, reading comprehension and other such areas. Specifically, however, the reading program was designed to suit the particular needs of the group, and wherever possible, the child. The reading program was related to other language art skills such as writing, spelling, listening, etc.

In group II, Tutorial Group Therapy (hereafter referred to as RG II), as in RG I, the subjects were told that they had been referred to the Clinic by their Probation Officers because of their reading difficulties. They were then told, however, that the therapist was not going to teach them to read, but rather, would try to help them to discover what could have interfered with their ability to learn to read. In essence, while they were encouraged to speak about early school experiences, attitudes toward teachers and attitudes toward reading, they were free to discuss any other matter. The therapist also indicated that they were free to make use of the reading material located in the room. The group was told that they could use the meetings as they saw fit—they could "talk" or "read." If the group chose to "talk" the meetings were conducted along formal therapeutic lines. If, on the other hand, they decided to "read," the therapist utilized remedial techniques appropriate to their individual reading needs. The emphasis, however, was always on the emotional concomitants of the reading process.

For example, if a child "got stuck" while reading something to the group, he was asked to describe how he felt at that particular moment; to try to recall similar situations in school; and to try to relate past experiences to present performance. On such occasions the other members of the group were encouraged to relate some of their own experiences and difficulties related to the reading problem under discussion. Thus, the therapist, while providing remedial assistance, used the reading process as a means of stimulating group discussion. Remedial reading as utilized in this form of therapy serves three general purposes: 1) it anchors the therapy in a concrete problem which is meaningful to the child; 2) it offers concrete help which contributes to strengthening the child's ego, and 3) it serves as a means of promoting group discussion and release of emotional material to which therapist and members could respond.

In the Interview Therapy Group (hereafter referred to as RG III), the subjects were told that they had been referred to the Clinic by their Probation Officers because of their difficulties in the community. The children were told that they had been referred for treatment of their personal problems and that the group had been formed so that they could be helped by the therapist and one another. The therapist further told them that they could talk at the meetings about anything they wished. No mention was made of their reading difficulties. In general, the group therapy followed the psychoanalytic principles and procedures described by Slavson (115) and Peck (88).

Procedure in Treating Data

All the materials used in this study were examined to see if there were any statistically significant results. The quantitative and qualitative results are presented and analyzed in Chapter IV. In addition all the data were examined to determine the extent to which they support the Hypotheses stated in Chapter I. This material is presented and discussed in Chapter V.

CHAPTER IV

RESULTS

The Data and Their Treatment

THE STATISTICAL TREATMENT and interpretation of the data are presented under the following three headings: Intelligence; Reading Achievement and Psycho-social Adjustment. Throughout, analysis of variance, and wherever indicated "t" tests, were used to determine the significance of the differences between the groups on the basis of changes between pre-therapy and post-therapy measures.

Intelligence

The pre and post intelligence test results are presented in tabular form below.

Table V contains the IQ's of RGI. The pre treatment IQ's ranged from 71 to 88 with a mean of 79.7. The post treatment IQ's ranged from 74 to 114 with a mean of 88. As indicated, the average gain for the group was 8.3.

TABLE V
COMPARISON OF PRE AND POST IQ'S OF RGI*

Subject	Pre	Post	Difference
A	71	75	4
B	88	114	26
C	82	87	5
D	85	91	6
E	80	85	5
F	75	74	−1
G	77	90	13
Mean	79.7	88.0	8.3

*Group Remedial Reading.

Table VI shows the IQ changes in RG II. As indicated, the pre IQ's ranged from 65 to 95 with a mean IQ of 81. The post IQ's ranged from 60 to 110 with the mean at 90.1. The average IQ gain was 9.1.

TABLE VI
COMPARISON OF PRE AND POST IQ's OF RG II*

Subject	Pre	Post	Difference
A	95	82	−13
B	79	87	8
C	65	60	−5
D	83	110	27
E	80	91	11
F	90	106	16
G	75	95	20
Mean	81.0	90.1	9.1

*Tutorial Group Therapy.

The IQ changes for RG III are shown in Table VII. In this group the pre treatment range was 72 to 87 and the mean 77.5. At the end of treatment the IQ's ranged from 68 to 96 with the mean being 82.0. The mean gain was found to be 4.4.

TABLE VII
COMPARISON OF PRE AND POST IQ's OF RG III*

Subject	Pre	Post	Difference
A	72	84	12
B	83	84	1
C	75	71	−4
D	87	87	0
E	72	96	24
F	74	68	−6
G	80	84	4
Mean	77.5	82.0	4.4

*Interview Group Therapy.

Table VIII presents a comparison of the average IQ gain for the three groups. As indicated, RG II showed the greatest gain although only slightly greater than RG I. The smallest gain occurs in RG III.

TABLE VIII
COMPARISON OF IQ GAIN FOR THE THREE GROUPS

Group	Pre Mean IQ	Post Mean IQ	Mean IQ Gain
RG I	79.7	88.0	8.3
RG II	81.0	90.1	9.1
RG III	77.5	82.0	4.4

The significance of the differences between the mean IQ gains was examined by an analysis of variance. The results, epitomized in Table IX, indicate no significant differences.

TABLE IX
SUMMARY OF ANALYSIS OF VARIANCE FOR IQ GAIN

Source	E Squares	df	Mean Square	F
Between groups	88.29	2	44.15	N.S.*
Within groups	681.61	6	113.60	N.S.
Residual	1616.39	12	134.70	
Total	2386.29	20		

*Below 5% level of confidence.

Reading Achievement

The pre and post treatment reading achievement test results are presented in tabular form below, and are based on the Gray's oral reading grade.

Table X reflects the pre and post data for RG I. As shown, the reading grades before treatment ranged from 1.0 to 5.4 with a mean grade of 2.8. After treatment the reading scores ranged from 1.0 to 6.1 with the mean at 3.9. Thus the group gained an average of 1.1 grades in reading.

TABLE X
COMPARISON OF PRE AND POST READING GRADES OF RG I*

Subject	Pre	Post	Difference
A	1.0	1.0	0
B	4.4	6.1	1.7
C	1.0	3.2	2.2
D	4.5	5.9	1.4
E	2.0	3.7	1.7
F	5.4	6.0	.6
G	1.4	1.4	0
Mean	2.8	3.9	1.1

*Group Remedial Reading.

The changes in reading effected by Tutorial Group Therapy are indicated in Table XI. It can be seen that the pre-therapy scores ranged from 1.0 to 4.9 and that the pre mean was 2.4. After treatment, the reading grades ranged from 2.3 to 6.4 with the mean falling at 4.2. The mean group gain was 1.8 grades in reading.

TABLE XI

COMPARISON OF PRE AND POST READING GRADES FOR RG II*

Subject	Pre	Post	Difference
A	1.0	2.6	1.6
B	1.0	4.0	3.0
C	3.7	3.9	.2
D	3.1	5.4	2.3
E	1.0	2.3	1.3
F	4.9	6.4	1.5
G	2.4	5.1	2.7
Mean	2.4	4.2	1.8

*Tutorial Group Therapy.

Table XII contains the reading test results for RG III. In this group the pre scores ranged from 1.0 to 4.4 with a mean of 2.8. After therapy, the reading scores ranged from 1.0 to 5.9 with a mean of 3.5. Thus the mean gain for RG III was .7 of a grade.

TABLE XII

COMPARISON OF PRE AND POST READING GRADES FOR RG III*

Subject	Pre	Post	Difference
A	3.1	3.4	.3
B	3.4	4.4	1.0
C	1.0	1.0	0
D	1.0	1.6	.6
E	4.4	4.5	.1
F	3.0	5.9	2.9
G	3.7	4.0	.3
Mean	2.8	3.5	.7

*Interview Group Therapy.

Figure 1 graphically compares the degree of reading gain for the three groups. The mean gain for each group was converted into a percentage by using the pre treatment mean as the denominator and the mean difference as the numerator. The obtained ratio was multiplied by 100 to yield the percentage gain for each group.

	100			
Per Cent Gain	80		74%	
	60			
	40	39%		
	20			26%
		RG I	RG II	RG III

Fig. 1. Comparison of reading gains based on pre and post means.

As illustrated in Figure I, RG II improved by 74% in reading as compared to an improvement of 39% for RG I and 26% for RG III. Thus the Tutorial Therapy Group showed a 35% greater improvement in reading than the Remedial Reading Group and a 48% greater gain than the Interview Therapy Group. In comparing RG I with RG III it can be seen that the Remedial Reading Group showed a 13% greater improvement than the Interview Therapy Group.

The significance of the differences among the mean reading gains for the three groups was examined by an analysis of variance (Table XIII). The results indicate that the differences between the Groups are not statistically significant (below 5% level of confidence). The Tutorial Therapy Group, nevertheless, showed a trend toward greater gain in reading than either of the other two groups.

TABLE XIII

SUMMARY OF ANALYSIS OF VARIANCE FOR PRE-POST READING GAIN

Source	*E Squares*	*df*	*Mean Square*	*F*
Between groups	407.23	2	203.61	N.S.
Within groups	396.13	6	66.02	N.S.
Residual	12,226.45	12	102.20	
Total	2,029.80	20		

Psycho-social Adjustment

Davidson Rorschach Signs

The pre and post treatment Davidson signs are presented below in tabular form. According to the criteria set up for this scale the greater the number of Rorschach signs, the better the adjustment. The maximum number of signs that could be obtained by any individual is 17.

The "pre" and "post" data for RG I is presented in Table XIV. Here we see that the "pre" scores for this group ranged from 3 to 8 with a mean adjustment score of 5.43. The post treatment scores ranged from 4 to 8 with a mean of 5.71. Thus the mean difference for the remedial reading group was .29 adjustment signs.

TABLE XIV

COMPARISON OF PRE-POST DAVIDSON RORSCHACH SIGNS FOR RG I*

Subject	Pre	Post	Difference
A	5	5	0
B	6	7	1
C	3	4	1
D	7	7	0
E	8	8	0
F	3	4	1
G	6	5	−1
Mean	5.43	5.71	.29

*Group Remedial Reading.

Table XV contains the "pre" and "post" adjustment signs for RG II. In this group the adjustment signs ranged from 3 to 7 before treatment and from 6 to 10 after treatment. The "pre" mean was 5.43 and the "post" mean 8.14. The group therefore showed a mean gain of 2.71 signs.

TABLE XV

COMPARISON OF PRE-POST DAVIDSON RORSCHACH SIGNS FOR RG II*

Subject	Pre	Post	Difference
A	5	9	4
B	5	9	4
C	6	6	0
D	3	7	4
E	7	7	0
F	7	10	3
G	5	9	4
Mean	5.43	8.14	2.71

*Tutorial Group Therapy.

The "pre" and "post" Rorschach signs for RG III are contained in Table XVI. From this table we see that the "pre" scores ranged from 4 to 8 and the "post" scores from 5 to 11. The "pre" mean was 5.85 and the "post" mean 8.0. Thus RG III, after treatment, showed a mean gain of 2.14 adjustment signs.

TABLE XVI

COMPARISON OF PRE-POST DAVIDSON RORSCHACH SIGNS FOR RG III*

Subject	Pre	Post	Difference
A	5	7	2
B	8	11	3
C	7	7	0
D	5	5	0
E	4	8	4
F	7	10	3
G	5	8	3
Mean	5.85	8.00	2.14

*Interview Group Therapy.

Figure 2 graphically compares the three groups in regard to percentage gain in adjustment. These data are based on the mean gain of each group on the Davidson Scale. The mean gain for each group was converted into a percentage by using the pre-treatment mean as the denominator and the difference between pre and post treatment means as the numerator. The obtained ratio was multiplied by 100 to yield the percentage gain.

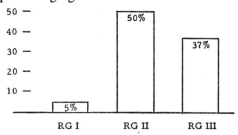

Fig. 2. Comparison of pre-post gain in adjustment based on Davidson's Rorschach signs.

As shown in Figure 2, RG II made the greatest gain in adjustment as measured by the Davidson Scale. In comparing the three groups we find that RG II shows a 45% greater improvement than RG I and a 13% greater improvement than RG III. Noteworthy is the finding that RG III showed a 32% greater improvement than RG I.

The significance of the differences among the mean gains of the Davidson Rorschach signs was examined by an analysis of variance. Table XVII epitomizes these findings and indicates that the variance between groups is significant at the 5% level.

TABLE XVII

Summary of Analysis of Variance for Pre-Post Adjustment Gain Based on the Davidson Rorschach Signs

Source	E Squares	df	Mean Square	F
Between groups	22.57	2	11.29	4.70*
Within groups	10.94	6	1.82	N.S.
Residual	28.78	12	2.40	
Total	62.29	20		

*Significant at 5% level.

Having thus determined that significant differences do exist between the groups, "t" tests were conducted in order to determine where the significant differences lay. Table XVIII contains the results of the "t" tests. In comparing RG II with RG I a "t" of 3.55 was obtained. This is significant at the 5% level of confidence. The difference between the amount of improvement shown for RG II and RG III was not significant. A "t" of 3.30, significant at the 5% level, was obtained in comparing RG I with RG III. In sum, then, RG II showed significantly greater improvement in adjustment than RG I, but no significant improvement over RG III.

TABLE XVIII

COMPARISON OF GROUP IMPROVEMENT IN ADJUSTMENT BASED
DAVIDSON RORSCHACH SIGNS

Comparison	Mean Gain$_1$	Mean Gain$_2$	Difference	t	Best Group
RG I vs. II	.29	2.71	2.42	3.55*	II
RG II vs. III	2.71	2.14	.57	N.S.	—
RG I vs. III	.29	2.14	1.85	3.30*	III

*Significant at 5% level.

Haggerty-Olson-Wickman Behavior Rating Scale Schedule B

The H.O.W. Behavior Rating Scale, Schedule B, consists of a graphic rating scale for each of thirty-five intellectual, physical, social and emotional traits. By use of H.O.W. the behavior status of a problem child may be designated in quantitative terms. The scale seems particularly suited for use in this study in that it allows for ratings in five areas of adjustment: intellectual, physical, social, emotional and total. Each subject was rated on the basis of his group behavior in the initial five sessions and in the last five sessions. The ratings were made by a trained phychologist who functioned as an observer in all group sessions.

Intellectual Ratings

Table XIX contains the H.O.W. results pre and post treatment for RG I in regard to intellectual adjustment. As shown, the "pre" scores ranged from 14 to 30 with the mean of 19.28. The "post" scores ranged from 12 to 26 with a mean of 18.28. Thus the remedial reading group showed a mean gain in this area of 1.00.

TABLE XIX
COMPARISON OF PRE-POST H.O.W.* INTELLECTUAL
ADJUSTMENT SCORES FOR RG I†

Subject	Pre	Post	Difference
A	30	26	−4
B	15	12	−3
C	21	21	0
D	19	22	3
E	14	15	1
F	15	14	−1
G	21	18	−3

*The lower the scale the better the adjustment.
†Group Remedial Reading.

The "pre-post" data on RG II is presented in Table XX. Here we see that the "pre" scores ranged from 15 to 31 while the "post" scores ranged from 10 to 19. The difference between the "pre" mean of 23.86 and the "post" mean of 14.70 reflects a mean gain of 9.16 in the area of intellectual adjustment.

TABLE XX
COMPARISON OF PRE-POST H.O.W.* INTELLECTUAL
ADJUSTMENT SCALE SCORES FOR RG II†

Subject	Pre	Post	Difference
A	24	17	−7
B	28	16	−12
C	22	19	−3
D	19	12	−7
E	28	13	−15
F	31	16	−15
G	15	10	−5
Mean	23.86	14.70	−9.16

*The lower the score the better the adjustment.
†Tutorial Group Therapy.

The "pre-post" changes for RG III are depicted in Table XXI. In this group the range changed from 15 to 28 before treatment to 13 to 23 after treatment. The "pre" mean was 22.43 and the "post" mean 18.57. Thus RG III showed a mean gain of 3.86.

TABLE XXI

COMPARISON OF PRE-POST H.O.W.* INTELLECTUAL ADJUSTMENT SCALE SCORES FOR RG III†

Subject	Pre	Post	Difference
A	15	15	0
B	24	19	−4
C	27	22	−5
D	28	23	−5
E	21	17	−4
F	17	13	−4
G	25	21	−4
Mean	22.43	18.57	−3.86

*The lower the score the better the adjustment.
†Interview Group Therapy.

For ease of comparison, the mean gain for each group was converted into a percentage. The comparison of the percentage gain for each group is graphically illustrated in Figure 3. In terms of intellectual adjustment RG I improved by 5%; RG II improved by 38%; and RG III showed an improvement of 21%. It is shown (Fig. 3) that RG II made the greatest improvement in the H.O.W. Intellectual Scale. RG II showed a 33% greater improvement than RG I and a 17% greater improvement than RG III. RG III showed a 16% greater improvement than RG I.

RG I—Group Remedial Reading
RG II—Tutorial Group Therapy
RG III—Interview Group Therapy

```
              50
              40              38%
Per Cent      30
  Gain        20                        21%
              10
                    5%
```

RG I	RG II	RG III

Fig. 3. Comparison of gain on H.O.W. intellectual adjustment Scale (based on pre and post means).

In order to determine whether any or all of the above differences are significant, the "pre-post" data was examined by an analysis of variance. The obtained F of 12.27 indicates that the differences between groups are significant at the 1% level. Table XXII summarizes the analysis of variance on the H.O.W. Intellectual Scale data.

TABLE XXII

SUMMARY OF ANALYSIS VARIANCE FOR PRE-POST GAINS ON H.O.W. INTELLECTUAL ADJUSTMENT SCALE

Source	E Squares	df	Mean Square	F
Between groups	242.66	2	121.33	12.27*
Within Groups	41.89	6	6.98	N.S.
Residual	118.69	12	9.89	
Total	403.24	20		

*Significant at 1% level.

Table XXIII contains the results of "t" tests which were conducted to determine the significance of the differences between the specific groups under examination. As shown, a "t" of 4.00 was obtained in comparing RG I with RG II, and this "t" is significant at the 1% level. In comparing RG I with RG III a "t" of 3.39 was obtained and this is significant at the 5% level. Lastly, in comparing RG II with RG III a "t" of 4.29 was obtained and this was found to be significant at the 1% level. Thus, RG II showed significantly greater gain on the H.O.W. Intellectual Scale than both RG I and RG II. Of note, is the finding that RG III was rated significantly better than RG I.

TABLE XXIII

COMPARISON OF GROUP IMPROVEMENT IN ADJUSTMENT BASED ON THE H.O.W. INTELLECTUAL SCALE, SCHEDULE B

Comparison	Mean Gain$_1$	Mean Gain$_2$	t	Best Group
RG I vs. RG II	1.00	9.16	4.00*	II
RG II vs. RG III	9.16	3.86	4.29*	II
RG I vs. RG III	1.00	3.86	3.39†	III

*Significant at 1% level.
†Significant at 5% level.

Physical Ratings

Table XXIV contains the results of the pre-post ratings on the H.O.W. Physical Scale for RG I. On this scale the pre scores ranged from 12 to 18 with a mean of 15.0. The post scores ranged from 11 to 17 with a mean of 13.71. Thus RG I showed a mean gain of 1.29 in physical adjustment.

TABLE XXIV

COMPARISON OF PRE-POST SCORES ON H.O.W.* PHYSICAL ADJUSTMENT SCALE FOR RGI†

Subject	Pre	Post	Difference
A	18	17	−1
B	12	12	0
C	16	11	−5
D	13	13	0
E	16	17	1
F	13	12	−1
G	17	14	−3
Mean	15.00	13.71	−1.29

*The lower the score the better the adjustment.
†Group Remedial Reading.

The data for RG II, pre and post treatment, are presented in Table XXV. This group ranged from 10 to 24 before treatment and from 11 to 18 after treatment. The "pre" mean was 17.55 and the "post" treatment mean was 14.10. Thus, RG II showed a mean gain of 3.45 in physical adjustment.

TABLE XXV

COMPARISON OF PRE-POST SCORES ON H.O.W.* PHYSICAL
ADJUSTMENT SCALE FOR RG II†

Subject	Pre	Post	Difference
A	19	16	−3
B	23	12	−11
C	14	15	1
D	17	12	−5
E	18	15	−3
F	24	18	−6
G	10	11	1
Mean	17.55	14.10	−3.45

*The lower the score the better the adjustment.
†Tutorial Group Therapy.

Table XXVI contains the "pre-post" results for RG III in regard to physical adjustment. The "pre" range for this group was 11 to 22 and the "post" range 11 to 20. The difference between the "pre" mean of 17.14 and the "post" mean of 15.85 is 1.29.

TABLE XXVI

COMPARISON OF PRE-POST SCORES ON H.O.W.* PHYSICAL
ADJUSTMENT SCALE FOR RE III†

Subject	Pre	Post	Difference
A	11	11	0
B	22	20	−2
C	21	15	−6
D	18	19	1
E	18	18	0
F	15	14	−1
G	15	14	−1
Mean	17.14	15.85	−1.29

*The lower the score the better the adjustment.
†Interview Group Therapy.

The "pre-post" mean gains for each group were converted into precentages and compared as shown in Figure 4.

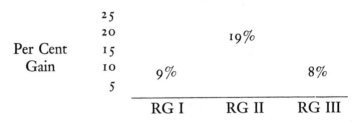

Fig. 4. Comparison of gain on H.O.W. physical adjustment scale (based on pre and post means).

Figure 4 illustrates the differences among the mean gains of each group in regard to physical adjustment. RG II shows a 10% greater improvement than RG I and an 11% greater improvement than RG III. The difference between RG I and RG III is only 1% with RG I showing the greater positive change. Thus, in comparing the three groups RG II shows the greatest gain in physical adjustment. In order to determine whether the above indicated differences were significant the data were examined by analysis of variance. The results of the analysis of variance are summarized in Table XXVII. As indicated, the differences between the mean gains for the three groups was found to be not significant.

TABLE XXVII

SUMMARY OF ANALYSIS OF VARIANCE FOR PRE-POST GAIN ON THE H.O.W. PHYSICAL ADJUSTMENT SCALE

Source	E Squares	df	Mean Square	F
Between groups	27.52	2	13.76	N.S.
Within groups	33.79	6	5.63	N.S.
Residual	128.50	12	10.71	
Total	189.81	20		

Social Adjustment

Table XXVIII contains the pre-post results on the H.O.W. Social Adjustment Scale for RG I, RG II and RG III respectively.

The pre scores for RG I ranged from 24 to 40, with a mean of 32.00. The post scores ranged from 18 to 32 with a mean of 27.42. Thus RG I showed a mean gain of 4.58 in social adjustment as measured by the H.O.W. Social Adjustment Scale.

TABLE XXVIII

COMPARISON OF PRE-POST SCORES ON THE H.O.W.* SOCIAL ADJUSTMENT SCALE

RG I—GROUP REMEDIAL READING

Subject	Pre	Post	Difference
A	31	28	−3
B	24	18	−6
C	40	30	−10
D	37	32	−5
E	37	31	−6
F	26	26	0
G	29	27	−2
Mean	32.00	27.42	−4.58

RG II—TUTORIAL GROUP THERAPY

Subject	Pre	Post	Difference
A	43	32	−9
B	45	26	−19
C	26	24	−2
D	25	18	−7
E	46	31	−15
F	37	19	−18
G	25	16	−9
Mean	35.28	23.70	−11.58

RG III—Interview Group Therapy

Subject	Pre	Post	Difference
A	28	27	−1
B	38	33	−5
C	27	21	−6
D	38	33	−5
E	27	29	2
F	26	25	−1
G	34	23	−11
Mean	31.14	27.28	−3.86

*The lower the score the better the adjustment.

RG II had a range of 25 to 46 before treatment and a range of 16 to 32 after treatment. The pre mean for this group was 35.28 and the post mean 23.70. Thus RG II manifested a mean gain of 11.58 on the H.O.W. Social Adjustment Scale.

The pre range for RG III was 26 to 38 with a mean of 31.14. The post range was 21 to 33 with a mean of 27.28. The mean gain for RG III was 3.86.

Figure 5 graphically depicts the mean gain for each group in terms of per cent gain in social adjustment.

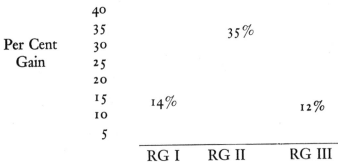

RG I—Group Remedial Reading
RG II—Tutorial Group Therapy
RG III— Interview Group Therapy

Per Cent Gain

40
35   35%
30
25
20
15   14%   12%
10
5

RG I   RG II   RG III

Fig. 5. Comparison of gain on H.O.W. social adjustment scale (based on pre and post means).

In comparing the three groups we find that RG II shows the greatest improvement in social adjustment. Figure 5 illustrates that RG II made a 19% greater improvement in social adjustment than RG I and 21% greater improvement than RG III. In order to determine the significance of the differences among the mean gains of the three groups, the above illustrated data was subjected to an analysis of variance. The results of the F test are summarized in Table XXIX. As shown the differences between groups are significant at the 5% level of confidence.

TABLE XXIX
SUMMARY OF ANALYSIS OF VARIANCE FOR PRE-POST GAIN ON THE H.OW. SOCIAL ADJUSTMENT SCALE

Source	Sum of Squares	df	Mean Square	F
Between groups	266.01	2	133.00	4.86*
Within groups	46.46	6	7.74	N.S.
Residual	328.57	12	27.38	
Total	641.04	20		

*Significant at 5% level.

In regard to the H.O.W. Social Adjustment Scale, using "t" tests, the difference between RG II and RG I was significant at the 5% level; the difference between RG II and RG III was significant at the 5% level; and the difference between RG I and RG III was not statistically significant. The t's for the three comparisons are presented in Table XXX.

TABLE XXX
COMPARISON OF GROUP IMPROVEMENT IN ADJUSTMENT BASED ON THE H.O.W. SOCIAL SCALE—SCHEDULE B

Comparison	Mean Gain$_1$	Mean Gain$_2$	t	Best Group
RG I vs. RG II	4.58	11.58	3.69*	II
RG II vs. RG III	11.58	3.86	3.09*	II
RG I vs. RG III	4.58	3.86	N.S.	—

*Significant at 5% level.

Emotional Ratings

Table XXXI contains the results of the pre-post H.O.W. Emotional Adjustment Scale for all three groups.

RG I shows a pre range of 24 to 43 with a mean of 37.00. The post scores ranged from 19 to 35 with a mean of 29.57. As indicated in Table XXXI, RG I effected a mean gain of 7.43 in emotional adjustment.

TABLE XXXI

COMPARISON OF PRE-POST SCORES ON H.O.W.* EMOTIONAL ADJUSTMENT SCALE

RG I—GROUP REMEDIAL READING

Subject	Pre	Post	Difference
A	43	35	−8
B	24	19	−5
C	43	30	−13
D	39	35	−4
E	29	30	1
F	25	25	0
G	28	33	5
Mean	37.00	29.57	−7.43

RG II—TUTORIAL GROUP THERAPY

Subject	Pre	Post	Difference
A	49	36	−13
B	47	22	−25
C	43	24	−19
D	28	18	−10
E	47	31	−16
F	40	19	−21
G	25	16	−9
Mean	39.85	23.70	−16.15

RG III—INTERVIEW GROUP THERAPY

Subject	Pre	Post	Difference
A	31	23	−8
B	45	35	−10
C	35	27	−8
D	43	42	−1
E	35	32	−3
F	28	22	−6
G	45	34	−11
Mean	37.43	30.71	−6.72

*The lower the score the better the adjustment.

RG II had a pre treatment range of 25 to 49 with a mean score of 39.85. After treatment this group had a range of 16 to 36 and a mean of 23.70. Thus RG II effected a mean gain of 16.15 in emotional adjustment.

RG III shows a pre treatment range of 28 to 45 and a pre treatment mean of 37.43. After treatment the scores ranged from 22 to 42 with a mean of 30.71. Thus the mean gain for RG III was 6.72.

In order to compare the degree of improvement effected by each group the mean gains were converted into percentages. Figure 6 graphically illustrates the differences between the groups on the H.O.W. Emotional Adjustment Scale.

RG I   - Group Remedial Reading
RG II   - Tutorial Group Therapy
RG III - Interview Group Therapy

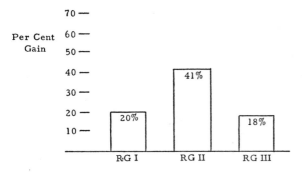

Fig. 6. Comparison of gain on the H.O.W. emotional adjustment scale (based on pre and post means).

As illustrated in Figure 6, RG II showed a 21% greater gain in emotional adjustment than RG I and 23% greater improvement than RG III. The difference in percentage gain in emotional adjustment between RG I and RG III is 2%, with RG I showing the greater improvement.

In order to determine whether the differences among the mean gains of the three groups were significant, the data were examined by means of analysis of variance. The results of the analysis of variance are summarized in Table XXXII. As indicated below the differences between the groups are significant at the 1% level of confidence.

TABLE XXXII

SUMMARY OF ANALYSIS OF VARIANCE FOR PRE-POST GAIN ON THE H.O.W. EMOTIONAL ADJUSTMENT SCALE

Source	Sum of Squares	df	Mean Square	F
Between groups	609.81	2	304.91	13.34*
Within groups	215.79	6	35.97	N.S.
Residual	274.21	12	22.85	
Total	1099.81	20		

*Significant at 1% level.

In regard to the H.O.W. Emotional Adjustment Scale, using "t" tests, the differences between RG I and RG II was significant at the 1% level, with RG II being the superior group. The difference between the improvements effected by RG II and RG III were also significant at the 1% level. The difference between RG I and RG III was not statistically significant. Thus RG II showed the greatest improvement in emotional adjustment and the degree of improvement effected by RG II when compared with each of the other two groups was found to be significant at the 1% level. The t's for the three comparisons are presented in Table XXXIII.

TABLE XXXIII

COMPARISON OF GROUP IMPROVEMENT IN ADJUSTMENT BASED ON THE H.O.W. EMOTIONAL ADJUSTMENT SCALE—SCHEDULE B

Comparison	Mean Gain$_1$	Mean Gain$_2$	t	Best Group
RG I vs. RG II	7.43	16.15	4.02*	II
RG I vs. RG III	7.43	6.72	N.S.	—
RG II vs. RG III	16.15	6.72	4.51*	II

*Significant at the 1% level.

Total Adjustment

Table XXXIV contains the results of the pre-post H. O. W. Total Adjustment Scale for all three groups.

The pre scores for RG I ranged from 75 to 120 with a mean of 99.28. The post scores for RG I ranged from 61 to 106 with a mean of 89.00. The mean gain for this group, in regard to the total scale was 10.28.

TABLE XXXIV

COMPARISON OF PRE AND POST SCORES ON THE H.O.W.* TOTAL ADJUSTMENT SCALE

Subject	Pre	Post	Difference
RG I—GROUP REMEDIAL READING			
A	122	106	−16
B	75	61	−14
C	120	92	−28
D	108	102	−6
E	96	93	−3
F	79	77	−2
G	95	92	−3
Mean	99.28	89.00	−10.28
RG II—TUTORIAL GROUP THERAPY			
A	135	101	−34
B	143	76	−67
C	105	82	−23
D	89	58	−31
E	139	85	−54
F	132	79	−53
G	75	53	−22
Mean	116.85	76.28	−40.57
RG III—INTERVIEW GROUP THERAPY			
A	85	76	−9
B	129	107	−22
C	110	85	−25
D	127	117	−10
E	101	96	−5
F	86	74	−11
G	119	92	−27
Mean	108.14	92.42	−15.72

*The lower the score the better the adjustment.

RG II had a pre treatment range of 75 to 143 with a mean of 116.85. After treatment the scores ranged from 53 to 101 with a mean of 76.28. Thus, RG II effected a mean gain of 40.57 in the H. O. W. Total Adjustment Scale.

The pre range for RG III was 85 to 129 with a mean of 108.14. The post range for RG III was 74 to 117 with a mean of 92.42. The mean gain for this group was 15.72.

The three groups were compared in regard to total adjustment by converting the mean gains for each group into a percentage. This figure, called percentage gain, was based on the difference between the pre and post means of the H. O. W. Total Adjustment Scale.

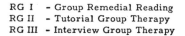

RG I   – Group Remedial Reading
RG II   – Tutorial Group Therapy
RG III – Interview Group Therapy

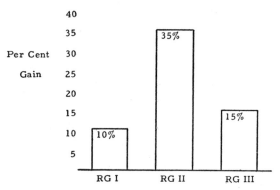

Fig. 7. Comparison of gain on the H.O.W. total adjustment scale (based on pre and post means).

As shown in Figure 7, RG II showed an over-all adjustment gain of 35%; RG III made a gain of 15%; and RG I effected an over all gain of 10%. The largest total gain was effected by RG II. The difference between RG I and RG II was 25% and a 20% difference is noted between RG II and RG III.

In order to determine whether the obtained differences among the mean gains of the three groups were significant, the data were examined by analysis of variance. Table XXXV contains the results of the analysis of variance which indicated that the differences between the groups were significant at the 1% level of confidence.

TABLE XXXV

SUMMARY OF ANALYSIS OF VARIANCE FOR PRE-POST GAIN ON THE H.O.W. TOTAL ADJUSTMENT SCALE—SCHEDULE B

Source	Sum of Squares	df	Mean Square	F
Between groups	3739.24	2	1869.62	9.47*
Within groups	785.12	6	130.85	N.S.
Residual	2049.45	12	170.79	
Total	6573.81	20		

*Significant at the 1% level.

In comparing the differences among the mean gains of the groups, using "t" tests, it was found that RG II's superiority over RG I in regard to Total Adjustment was significant at the 1% level. In comparing RG II with RG III, a "t" of 3.47 was obtained and this is significant at the 5% level. The difference between RG I and RG III was found to be statistically not significant. The t's for the three comparisons are presented in Table XXXVI.

TABLE XXXVI

COMPARISON OF GROUP IMPROVEMENT IN ADJUSTMENT BASED ON THE H.O.W. TOTAL ADJUSTMENT SCALE—SCHEDULE B

Comparison	Mean Gain$_1$	Mean Gain$_2$	t	Best Group
RG I vs. RG II	10.28	40.57	4.13*	II
RG I vs. RG III	10.28	15.72	N.S.	—
RG II vs. RG III	40.57	15.72	3.47†	II

*Significant at 1% level.
†Significant at 5% level.

SUMMARY CHART OF TEST FINDINGS

Productivity (Rorschach)

Meager	Average	Rich and well ordered	Rich, but chaotic	Chaotic

Relation to Reality (Rorschach, WISC–CAS, Drawings)

Fanatical exactitude	Not noticeably disturbed	Firm and good	"Artistic leeway"	Loose

Usual–Unusual Thought Content (Rorschach, Drawings)

Stereotyped	Average	Original	Bizarre qualities offset by other features	Bizarre

Emotional Tone (Rorschach, Szondi)

Lacking Repressed	Struggling for Expression	Warm Readily available	Getting out of hand	Emotions rampant

Constructive Fantasy (Rorschach)

Absent	Average	Active	Active+	Topheavy, withdrawal

Passivity–Aggression (Rorschach, Szondi, Drawings)

Hampering passivity	Insufficient drive	Sufficient drive	Aggression+	Overpowering aggression

Fig. 8. Sample of summary chart.

Psychologists' Ratings

The projective tests of each subject were analyzed and personality "profiles" developed for each child before and after treatment. At this point it may be valuable to introduce the reader to the Summary Chart (53) which was used to integrate the projective test data and upon which the psychologists based their ratings of pre-post improvement. As will be noticed (Fig. 8) this chart enables us to place the subject who has been tested on a five point scale with regard to six areas:

His productiveness

His relation to reality

The quality of his thought processes

His emotional tone

The extent of his constructive fantasy

The amount of aggressiveness or passivity that was shown in the test findings.

Although there is a good deal of subjectivity in qualitative evaluations of psychological material, some guiding principles were established in order to increase the objectivity of scoring for the Summary Charts. Two psychologists, working collaboratively and checking each other's work, completed the Summary Charts a considerable time after testing had been completed and reports written. The reports and test protocols themselves were consulted; from these two sources came the material for the rating of the summary chart. At no time did the psychologists know whether they were rating pre or post treatment test findings, nor the experimental group to which the subject belonged.

Because of the nature of the population and the special testing problems encountered by psychologists in a court setting, it was decided to use a more relative approach to the question of Rorschach productivity and to use different norms than those usually applied to Rorschach protocols. Consequently, an "average" protocol in this study is one which has from 9 to 25 responses. Any protocol having less than 9 responses would, of course, be termed "meager." A "rich and well ordered" protocol is one which has over

25 responses and is generally adequate in sequence, type of response and over-all integratedness. A "rich, but chaotic" protocol is one having more than average number of responses, but showing disturbance in the pattern of reactivity, fluctuations in responsiveness to each individual Rorschach stimulus and/or other indications of disturbances affecting reactivity. The last sub-category, "chaotic," includes those protocols which show few vestiges of control of Rorschach reactivity and productivity.

The Rorschach, WISC-CAS and Figure Drawing Tests contributed to the evaluation of Relation to Reality. "Fanatical exactitude" is self-explanatory, "not noticeably disturbed" is differentiated from "firm and good" by indications of some minor degree of disturbance in reality contact which, nevertheless, falls within the "normal" range. Where contact was seen to be less than significantly disturbed ("which would be termed 'loose' "), but showed evidence of deviations from "normal" contact as well as restitutive features, it was classified as "artistic leeway."

The evaluation of thought content is difficult to describe. A "stereotyped" manner of thinking is, in this summary, one with limited flexibility or perseverative in nature, or otherwise circumscribed. A person showing originality is one who displays some capacity for thinking which, at least to some extent, shows him capable of being somewhat more constructive and/or self-directed than the average. A "bizarre" record is replete with evidences of deviant thinking; where it appeared to be attributable to some situational feature or did not seem to be deeply ingrained in the personality structure, it was scored "bizarre qualities offset by other features." All other protocols were called "Average."

The Rorschach and the Szondi entered into the consideration of the emotional tone of the subject. Where there was an absence of color reactivity on the Rorschach and a repressed paroxysmal vector on the Szondi (plus e, minus hy), the subject's affective life was considered repressed. A struggle over the expression of emotions was considered to be demonstrated by minimal affective reactivity in the face of indications of generally limited freedom of expression. Where there was evidence of a general freedom of emotional experience, the term "warm, readily available" was applied. The degree to which some controls on emotional expression was present permitted a differentiation between the last two subcategories, "getting out of hand" and "emotions rampant."

Where there was no M in the test record, constructive fantasy was adjudged absent. From 1 to 2 M merited the description "Average." If there were more than 2 M, the subject was considered to have an active fantasy life; as the total number of M increased in proportion to the size of the Rorschach protocol, greater fantasy activity and even withdrawal was indicated.

The total test record was consulted for the evaluation of the Passivity-Aggression continuum. The degree of reactivity, the type of reactivity, indications of passive and aggressive impulses and the degree to which the subjects accepted or rejected their passivity and aggressiveness, among other factors, were considered in the evaluation of this category.

After the pre and post summary charts were completed, three qualified psychologists were asked to serve as judges in order to evaluate the changes noted in the pre and post charts of each subject. The judges were asked to give a clinical estimate of the degree of change of all 21 subjects on the following scale:

Considerable Improvement	Partial Improvement	No Change	Worse
(+2)	(+1)	(0)	(−1)

Each of the judges had an M.A. degree in clinical

psychology and more than 3 years of experience in the evaluation of personality by means of projective techniques.

Table XXXVII contains the ratings of the three judges in regard to change evidenced in the Summary Chart of test findings. The reliability of the ratings is established by the finding of 90.50% agreement among judges. In view of the degree of reliability it was decided to average the ratings of the three judges in order to compare the differences among the three groups. The average total score for each subject was used as an index of over-all change and these data were examined by an analysis of variance (Table XXXVIII). An F of 17.16 was obtained, indicating that the differences among the three groups in terms of the psychologists' ratings of over-all improvement is significant at the 1% level of confidence.

TABLE XXXVIII

SUMMARY OF ANALYSIS OF VARIANCE FOR PSYCHOLOGISTS' RATINGS*
OF OVER-ALL IMPROVEMENT

Source	Sum of Squares	df	Mean Square	F
Between groups	64.88	2	32.44	17.16†
Within groups	17.40	6	2.90	N.S.
Residual	22.72	12	1.89	
Total	105.00	20		

*Based on average scores of three raters.
†Significant at 1% level.

In regard to the psychologists' ratings of over-all improvement, using "t" tests, the difference between RG I and RG II is significant at the 1% level; the difference between RG I and RG III is not significant; and the difference between RG II and RG III is significant at the 1% level. The t's for the three comparisons are presented in Table XXXIX. As shown, RG II showed significantly greater improvement after treatment than either RG I or RG III.

TABLE XXXVII

JUDGES' RATINGS* OF THE SUMMARY CHART

Category	Productivity			Relation to Reality			Thought Content			Emotional Tone			Constructive Fantasy			Passivity Aggression			Average Total
Judges:	1	2	3	1	2	3	1	2	3	1	2	3	1	2	3	1	2	3	
RG I A	0	0	0	-1	-1	-1	0	0	0	0	0	0	0	0	0	0	0	0	-1
B	0	0	0	0	0	0	0	0	0	-1	-1	-1	0	0	0	0	0	0	1
C	0	0	0	0	0	0	0	0	0	0	0	0	0	0	0	0	0	0	0
D	0	0	0	0	0	1	0	0	0	0	0	0	0	-1	0	0	0	0	-.33
E	0	0	0	-1	-1	0	0	0	0	0	0	0	0	0	0	1	1	1	2
F	0	0	0	0	0	1	0	0	0	0	0	0	0	0	0	1	1	1	1
G	0	0	0	0	0	0	0	0	0	0	0	0	0	0	0	0	0	0	0
RG II A	0	0	0	0	0	1	0	0	0	0	0	0	0	0	1	1	0	1	1
B	2	2	2	1	1	1	1	1	1	1	1	1	1	1	1	1	1	1	7
C	1	1	1	2	2	1	-1	-1	-1	0	0	0	1	1	1	1	1	1	3.66
D	1	1	1	1	0	1	1	1	-1	1	1	1	1	1	1	1	1	1	6
E	0	0	0	0	1	0	0	0	1	1	1	1	1	1	1	0	0	0	3
F	1	1	1	2	2	2	0	0	0	1	1	1	1	1	1	2	2	2	5
G	1	1	-1	1	1	1	-1	-1	-1	0	0	0	0	0	0	1	1	1	5
RG III A	1	0	1	1	1	1	-1	-1	-1	0	0	0	0	0	0	0	0	0	1.33
B	0	0	0	1	1	1	0	0	0	0	0	0	1	1	1	0	0	0	2
C	0	0	0	0	0	0	0	0	0	0	0	0	0	0	-1	0	0	0	-.33
D	0	0	0	-1	-1	-1	-1	-1	-1	-1	-1	-1	-1	0	1	0	0	0	0
E	1	1	1	0	0	0	0	0	0	0	0	0	0	0	0	0	0	0	1
F	1	1	1	1	1	0	0	0	0	1	1	1	-1	-1	-1	0	0	0	2.66
G	0	0	0	0	0	0	0	0	1	0	0	0	0	0	0	0	0	0	.33

Key: Considerable improvement (+2)
Partial improvement (+1)
No change (0)
Worse (−1)
*Reliability: 90.5% agreement.

TABLE XXXIX

COMPARISON OF GROUP IMPROVEMENT IN ADJUSTMENT BASED ON
PSYCHOLOGISTS RATINGS

Comparison	$Mean_1$	$Mean_2$	5	Best Group
RG I vs. RG II	.38	4.38	5.33*	II
RG I vs. RG III	.38	1.00	N.S.	—
RG II vs. RG III	4.38	1.00	4.51*	II

*Significant at 1% level.

Figure 9 contains the comparison of the three groups in regard to improvement evidenced on the Summary Chart of Test Findings. As was previously indicated, the judges rated each subject on a four point scale of improvement for six personality areas. The percentages of the subjects in each group falling into the categories of "partial improvement" and "considerable improvement?" were computed and compared by means of bar graphs (Fig. 9).

In regard to Productivity, 57% of the members of RG II were rated as improved as compared to 43% for RG III and 0% for RG I. While all of the members of RG I (100%) were rated "no change," only 43% of RG II and 57% of RG III were so rated. None of the subjects in the three groups were rated "worse."

The ratings for the category Relation to Reality show a similar trend. Here too, the greatest change was effected by RG II. As illustrated, 71% of the subjects in RG II were rated as improved; 43% of the subjects in RG III were rated as improved; and 0% of the subjects in RG I were rated as improved. In RG I, 86% of the subjects were rated "no change" and 14% rated "worse." While 29% of the subjects in RG II were rated "no change," none was rated as "worse." As far as RG III is concerned, 43% of the group rated "no change" and 14% "worse."

The findings with respect to the category Thought Content are as follows: 43% of RG II rated improved; 0% of RG III rated improved. All of the subjects (100%) in RG

I were rated "no change"; 43% of the subjects in RG II were rated "no change"; and 71% of the subjects in RG III were rated "no change." While none of the subjects in RG I was rated "worse," 14% of RG II and 29% of RG III were so rated.

In regard to Emotional Tone, 57% of the subjects in RG II, 14% of the subjects in RG I and 29% of the subjects in RG III were rated as improved. The percentages of subjects in each group rated "no change" are as follows: 86% of RG I; 43% of RG II; and 71% of RG III. None of the subjects in any of the groups were rated as "worse" in regard to this category.

The findings for the category Constructive Fantasy are as follows: all the subjects (100%) in RG I were rated "no change"; in regard to RG II, 86% of the subjects were rated as improved and 14% rated "no change"; 29% of RG III were rated as improved, 57% as "no change" and 14% as "worse." Thus, of the three groups, RG II shows the greatest improvement in the category Constructive Fantasy.

In terms of the category Passivity-Aggression, the greatest improvement took place in RG II. In RG II 86% of the subjects were rated improved and 14% were rated "no change." All of the members of RG III (100%) were rated "no change." In RG I, 29% of the members were rated as improved and 71% as "no change."

In sum then, RG II consistently showed greater improvement in all areas of the Summary Chart than either RG I or RG III. This qualitative trend evidenced by the ratings of pre-post Summary Charts of Test Findings tends to support the finding (Table XXXIX) that RG II effected significantly greater improvement in total adjustment than either of the two other experimental groups.

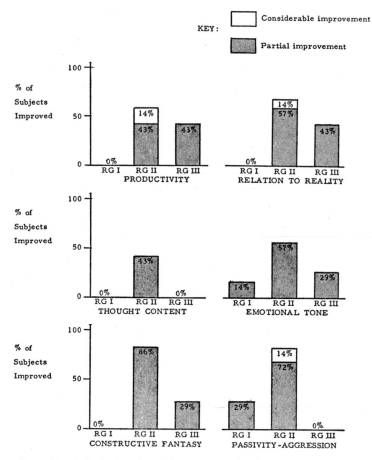

Fig. 9. Psychologists' rating of improvement in six personality areas.

Social Workers' Evaluations

At the conclusion of the experiment the case history of each subject was examined by a psychiatric social worker in order to investigate the changes in overt behavior. Apparent changes in interpersonal relationships, attitudes and behavior were noted. The social workers' evalulations were based on the following material which was available for each child: probation officer's investigation, school reports, and pre-treatment and post-treatment social worker interviews with child and parent.

At the end of the experimental period adjustment changes were evaluated in the following areas and sub-areas:

1. School
2. Home
   a. Parents
   b. Siblings
3. Community
   a. Legal
   b. Social
   c. Peer
   d. Authority
4. Emotional

Although these areas of possible change are obviously interrelated, they are sufficiently independent to permit analysis of each. It therefore seemed necessary to consider them separately as well as totally for clarity in making comparisons. The social workers were asked to evaluate each child, in the areas indicated above, on the following four point scale:

Considerable Improvement	Partial Improvement	No Change	Worse
(+2)	(+1)	(0)	(−1)

These evaluations were based on clinical judgment of trend and not on formal criteria. Thus, the social workers' evaluations permitted a breakdown into area of improvement on the one hand, and relative degree of improvement on the other.

Figure 10 contains the comparison of the three groups in regard to improvement as evaluated by the social workers. The percentages of the subjects in each group falling into the categories of "partial improvement" and "considerable improvement" were computed and compared by means of bar graphs.

In regard to school adjustment, 71% of the members of RG II were rated as improved as compared to 43% of RG I and 28% of RG III. While 28% of RG II were rated "no change," 57% of RG I and 28% of RG III were so rated. None of the members of RG II or RG I was rated "worse." However, 28% of RG III received the rating "worse" in regard to school adjustment. It is of interest to note that the trend toward better school adjustment as evidenced by the respective ranking of the three groups (II, I, III) corresponds with the trend toward greater gain in reading evidenced by the same ranking (II, I, III). Thus, the Tutorial Therapy Group, which manifested the greater gain in reading also shows a trend toward greater gain in school adjustment as evaluated by social workers.

The findings in the area of home adjustment are as follows: 86% of RG II were rated as improved and half of these rated as showing "considerable improvement"; 71% of RG III rated as improved and of these 28% as showing "considerable improvement"; 71% of RG I rated as improved with none of these being rated "considerable improvement." None of the subjects in the three groups received a rating of "worse" in this area of adjustment.

In regard to the category Parents—dealing with the degree of conflict evidenced in the subjects' relationship to their parents—no child was rated "worse." In RG II and RG I 86% were rated as improved and in RG III 71% were rated as improved. While 43% of RG II and 28% of RG III received the rating "considerable improvement," none of the members of RG I was so rated.

In terms of adjustment to siblings the groups show little difference in regard to trend toward improvement. In RG I, 57% were rated as showing "partial improvement," and none as showing "considerable improvement"; of the 57% in RG II rated as improved half evidenced "considerable improvement"; in RG III 43% rated "partial improvement" and 14% "considerable improvement."

In examining the differences between the groups in regard to community adjustment we find that 86% of RG II, 71% of RG I and 71% of RG III were rated as improved. In terms of degree of improvement 28% of RG I, 43% of RG II and 28% of RG III obtained the rating "considerable improvement." None of the subjects was rated as "worse."

It will be noted that the groups show a similar trend in the category of legal adjustment. This category had specific reference to the number of times, if any, a child was brought back to court on a new petition. In RG II and RG III 71% of the members were rated as improved and 57% of RG I were so rated. While 14% of RG I rated "worse," none of the subjects in either RG II or RG III received such a rating.

In terms of social adjustment, RG II shows the greatest gain with 86% of its members rated improved as compared to 71% so rated in RG I and RG III. This trend toward better social adjustment in RG II is further supported by comparing the relative degree of improvement evidenced in the three groups. In RG II 29% were rated as showing "considerable improvement," 57% "partial improvement," and 14% "no change." In RG I 14% rated "considerable improvement," 57% "partial improvement," 14% "no change," and 14% "worse." The distribution for RG III is as follows: 14% "considerable improvement," 57% "partial improvement," and 28% "no change."

In comparing the group with regard to changes in the area of peer relationships it was found that 71% of RG I and RG II were rated as improved while only 57% of RG III were so rated. Breaking this down to degree of improvement revealed that 14% of RG II and RG III were rated "considerable improvement" while no one in RG I was so rated. While none of the members of RG II or RG III was rated "worse," 14% of RG I were rated "worse" in regard to peer relationships.

In regard to attitude and adjustment to authority a clear trend toward greater improvement for the Tutorial Therapy Group is observable. In this respect 86% of RG II rated improved and half of this 86% as showing "considerable improvement." In RG III 71% rated improved and 28% of those so rated received an evaluation of "considerable improvement." As far as RG I is concerned 14% rated "considerable improvement" and 43% "partial improvement." It is of interest to note that no subject in any of the groups received a rating of "worse" in this particularly significant area of adjustment.

The last category evaluated by the social workers concerned the subjects' general emotional adjustment. The findings illustrated in Figure 10 (on following page) are as follows: 43% of RG I rated "partial improvement," 28% of RG II rated "considerable improvement," and 28% "partial improvement." The distribution of percentage of subjects improved for RG III is the same as that for RG II.

The social workers' judgments indicated that RG II, Tutorial Group Therapy, effected greater improvement in psycho-social adjustment than did either of the other two experimental groups. In order to determine the statistical significance of the differences between the three groups, the data were subjected to an analysis of variance test. Table XL Summarizes the results of the analysis of variance for the social workers' ratings of total improvement in psycho-social adjustment. As indicated below, differences between groups were found to be insignificant.

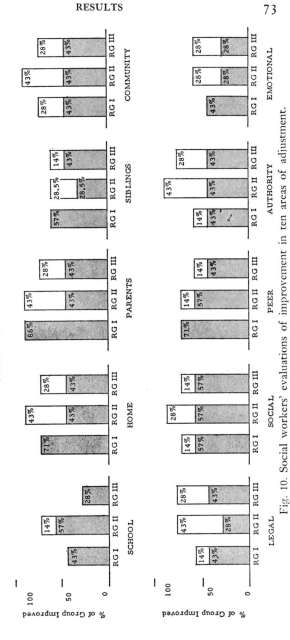

Fig. 10. Social workers' evaluations of improvement in ten areas of adjustment.

TABLE XL

SUMMARY OF ANALYSIS OF VARIANCE FOR SOCIAL WORKERS' RATINGS
OF TOTAL IMPROVEMENT IN PSYCHO-SOCIAL ADJUSTMENT

Source	Sum of Squares	df	Mean Square	F
Between groups	64.00	2	32.05	N.S.
Within groups	197.22	6	32.87	N.S.
Residual	409.93	12	34.16	N.S.
Total	671.24	20		

Qualitative Results

The organized and systematic study of treatment groups, be they remedial or therapeutic, involves many complex problems. It may be, for example, that some crucial aspects of group process cannot be communicated in objectively verifiable terms. In fact, as yet indefinable aspects of the therapist's or teacher's personality may be more important for his results than the technique he states he uses.

Assuming that objective study of group treatment is possible, major difficulties arise from the fact that the therapist is himself involved in the process he is observing. As his emotions and attitudes are inevitably involved in the treatment of his patients, his perceptions, observations and recordings are bound to be biased in some unknown manner. Furthermore, the effort to take notes during a group session, or to be somewhat preoccupied with remembering details for later recall and recording may impede the therapist's ability to function in a free and spontaneous manner. In view of the above considerations the present study relied heavily on data obtained from a specially trained observer who worked in close collaboration with the therapist conducting the three groups.

The psychologist who functioned as an observer in all three groups had three primary responsibilities: 1) recording from direct observation of group meetings the verbal and non-verbal communications exchanged; 2) conferring with the therapist immediately after each session, and 3) frequent discussion of the data obtained.

Clinical Overview of the Groups

The group meetings held at the clinic averaged an hour and a half. The observer and therapist spent half an hour in discussion after each meeting and (as the study developed) another half-hour preceding each meeting. Each session, therefore, took two and one-half hours. The time involved in recording the account of the meeting varied with the complexity of the session. Seldom, however, was it possible to complete the dictation in less than three hours.

A running account of each meeting was written by the observer, whose regular attendance enabled him to become familiar with the behavior patterns of the individual subjects, to follow the development of patterns of relationship within the group, and to obtain a clear perception of the therapists' attitudes and techniques. The running account was in essence an eye witness narrative of what was taking place in each group.

In addition a summary of each meeting was prepared by the therapist and observer, on the basis of the running account and the therapists' impressions. It selected out those aspects of the meeting which the therapist and observer agreed should be stressed. It contained references to previous meetings and goals and predictions for future meetings.

All of the group meetings were held in a large, airy room which was devoid of any ornamentation. During the meetings the observer sat at a short distance behind the semi-circle around which the therapist and subjects met. The observer was introduced to the groups at their first meeting and his role was described as follows:

Dr. Margolin is here to take notes on what we say and do.

None of this material will go to Court. It is all confidential and for our use in the Clinic. It may be helpful to all of us at some later date should we have some question about what went on in an early meeting.

Needless to say the acceptance of the above explanation varied from individual to individual. Initially, all were quite suspicious and hostile toward the observer. There were such comments as: "Does he write everything?" "Doesn't his hand get tired?" "Can't he talk?" etc. On one occasion he was greeted with, "Here comes our secretary." On another occasion he was subjected to a general attack by the group. It should be noted however that at no time did he become actively involved in any discussion. Occasionally, the group would look to the observer for a response when they might have called on the therapist, or when there was some conflict with the therapist. In such situations the observer referred them back to the therapist in an attempt to keep his own role and that of the therapist clearly distinguished in their minds. As the meetings progressed there was greater acceptance of the observer's presence, and, among many of the subjects, a clearly positive attitude was expressed toward him.

Certain of the phenomena that were observed in the early group meetings appeared to have significance for the entire course of treatment in each group. The salient features of the first few meetings in all of our groups was the stress felt by the subjects, primarily because the meetings were held within the Court building and because of their uncertainty about what to expect.

The therapist in working with these groups was faced with a paradox familiar to all who have worked with delinquents. These children reached the Court because of certain characteristic disturbances in their relations with authority which made it practically impossible to treat them in any other setting; yet the court setting, in itself, seemed to intensify their previously formed patterns of defense to such a degree as to create an almost insurmountable resistance to treatment. Resistance, of course, may serve as the therapists' first foothold. But before it can be utilized as a means of involving the patient, it must first be correctly diagnosed and understood by the therapist and made apparent to the patient through the medium of the relationship. In general, it is extremely difficult in the individual treatment of delinquents to bring the resistance into the open and to resolve it. Within the first few group sessions of this study, however, characteristic aspects of resistance were externalized and expressed with considerable directness. While this was quite encouraging, it was sometimes difficult for the therapist to direct and utilize. The nature of the resistances expressed and their subsequent direction seemed to be intrinsically related to the structure and purpose of the group and the specific therapeutic techniques used.

The following summaries may help to show the early manifestation of resistance in each of the three group settings and how the different group techniques inhibited or facilitated the establishment of mores favorable to treatment in a threatening and authoritative setting.

RG I—Group Remedial Reading

Summary of Meeting No. 1—RG I: The group seemed at a loss for a brief period at the beginning of the meeting but very soon all of the members seemed to perceive the situation as analogous to school and responded accordingly. In this classroom atmosphere the members related primarily to the therapist (as a teacher) and in a generally passive and conforming manner. This continued throughout the meeting which was marked by a lack of spontaneity. At all times the group waited for further instructions even to not drinking their cokes until the "order" was given. It should be noted that the nature of their tasks and the procedures employed by the therapist properly contributed to this atmosphere.

The only exception was that of Bob who briefly challenged the therapist almost immediately after his entry. Even he soon complied to the group norm when the therapist accepted his need to establish status. There appeared to be some indirect competition between members during this meeting. The only sign of interaction being in the group's slight concern over the attention given to Richard which was partially compensated for by his evident need for help.

It is also interesting to note that the sharing of material was perceived by the group as a strictly mechanical rather than cooperative process. It may be possible to learn something of the nature of schoolroom process from the behavior and attitudes reflected in this structured group.

Summary of Meeting No. 2—RG I: The group began with less caution and reserve than evidenced at the beginning of the last meeting. Ed was the only one who sought to please the therapist consistently throughout the session. The reserve of the others disappeared toward the middle of the meeting and Joe as well as Bob attempted to relate more closely to the therapist.

There was considerable concern over who the therapist was talking to and some annoyance over the attention given to Richard. Toward the end of the meeting, despite the therapists' effort to keep participation units short and to the point, there was some reduction of interest and marked centrifugal pressure, primarily from Bob and Charles who left the room to smoke and seemed impatient as had Ralph and Joe. This resistance seems to be primarily directed toward the task rather than the therapist toward whom they respond in a positive manner. Despite the therapists' permissiveness he is still viewed as a teacher in an authoritative setting (note incident when Bob and

Charles anticipated being reprimanded for smoking; then surprise at "teacher's" acceptance).

There has been some evidence of increase in interaction between the members: 1) Bob and Charles we have noted; 2) the contact between Ed and Richard involved Ed taking at first a somewhat patronizing pleasure in helping Richard with gradual growing resentment by Richard; 3) Ed's open refusal to work cooperatively with Bob; 4) the sharing of confidences among Joe, Ralph and Harold, and 5) Joe's offering to help Ralph with his reading.

Thus we have a group structure in which centrifugality and acting out tendencies are centered in Bob and Charles. Richard remains helpless but with some irritation in the role. Ed continues to be primarily therapist oriented, pleasing and conforming, while Joe, Ralph and Harold play a quiet, somewhat peripheral role.

The group continues to have very little spontaneity or self starting quality. The group's ability to deal with their underlying resistance to reading seems to derive essentially from the therapists' personal warmth and his utilization of interesting teaching techniques which require group involvement.

As the meetings progressed the group began to assume greater structure and there was increasing evidence of a need to deal with personal problems which were not directly related to the remedial activities. In keeping with the experimental design, however, all non-task oriented discussions were discouraged.

Summary of Meeting No. 6—RG I: The group has begun to reflect differences in ability with Joe and Bob somewhat better in reading than the others. There also has developed (especially clear in this meeting) specific cliques which are seemingly related to reading level and "antisocial status." It is of interest to note that Ed and Richard form one clique and Bob and Charles another.

The sub-groups are quite similar in attitude and level of

emotional maturity. Ed and Richard have formed extremely dependent relationships with the therapist. Ed in particular constantly "demands" therapists' support and approval. Bob and Charles manifest an acting out of a more directly aggressive pattern. Joe remains essentially solitary and conforming. Ralph and Harold continue in a peripheral role.

The group still relates to the therapist as "teacher." They relax when he leaves the room and they continue to structure the group like a classroom. The tension level remains low except when projected material emerges and here the anxiety is handled through laughter.

There appears to be a good deal of emotionally-laden material just below the surface that has been seeping through in their writing of stories. The stories created by the group are specifically used for remedial purposes and none of the material is probed or interpreted.

It seems as though the group members (especially Charles and Ed) are trying to communicate some of their emotional problems to the therapist through the limited channels available in this type of group. In any event their story projections reflect the characteristic behavior pattern of each of the members.

There has been considerable verbal exchange among the group members. The channels for intra-group communication are fairly open, in spite of the fact that the group is primarily task oriented.

RG II—Tutorial Group Therapy

Summary of Meeting No. 1—RG II: This meeting was highlighted by the sharp change in the group's attitude from complete resistance to learning and school to an almost pathetic desire to learn to read a little better than they can at the present time. The change was marked by a steady increase in interest in the utility of reading and in the mechanics thereof as the therapist made them more attractive (perhaps for the first time).

The therapist emphasized repeatedly by noting their own comments that their ability to read involved volition and attitude rather than "inability." At no time did the therapist question their ability to learn and he consistently offered considerable ego support. Throughout the meeting he seemed interested in the members as people rather than in their ability to read or learn.

Initially there was a unanimous resistance to learning. However, as Al maintained his facade, James and Tony came to the therapist's assistance by pressuring Al with regard to the difficulties he would encounter by not being able to read. Tony led the group through the last stages of change of attitude when he stated after Al had insisted almost desperately that he did not want to learn that he, "Tony," "wanted to try." The group's resistance collapsed after this and all that remained was their admitting in turn of their underlying desire to learn and the opening of a path toward this goal.

There was little interaction between the members except for the pressure on Al by Tony and James as noted above. Most of the communication was through the therapist.

Summary of Meeting No. 2—RG II: The meeting began with a brief resentment of the contest over whether a permissive atmosphere with some spontaneity was to be the rule or a classroom atmosphere was to reign. The situation was quickly resolved when the therapist refused to play the role of teacher as was suggested but did help the group to get started.

During much of the meeting the group relaxed and experienced a more spontaneous situation, being helped through the unfamiliarity of a permissive situation by the therapist's guilessness and acceptance of their content and their testing of him. This reached its peak when Tony challenged the therapist to leave the role of interrogator and give his thoughts, which the therapist seemed to do at the moment. At the end of the meeting the group seemed much freer and spontaneous and were beginning to offer more lengthy, complex comments, many of which were unsolicited.

The therapist felt, at the conclusion of the meeting, that while this meeting was essentially an interview session with some establishment of analytic mores—that it was also setting up a readiness for remedial work, e.g., their return to attitudes regarding their need to learn to read.

It should be noted that Tony's testing out of the "teacher role of the therapist" is of significance and interest in this form of group therapy. It is quite likely that at some future date, the attitude will arise to the effect that "He is a teacher but a different kind of teacher." At this point the group realizes that they are free to discuss what they wish and that this "teacher" is willing to accept and recognize their feelings. Furthermore, the therapist has shown them that he can concretely help them in reading and that he knows something about why they have not been able to learn to read. It is likely that this attitude will be generalized to other areas, so that we may expect in the future a group attitude which signifies: "If he helped me in reading and knew about these things, maybe he can help me with some of my other problems."

Much of the content during all of these initial discussions will be of therapeutic use later on: when a member experiences difficulty in future group reading and evidences his reaction to frustration, one can point out the consistent patterns of behavior relating to learning and deal with these rather than with his specific reading error.

The members have begun to relate more to each other and while the therapist remains the hub of the group, different roles are beginning to emerge. Tony, whose feelings are closest to the surface and who is most capable of verbalizing, takes the lead in introducing new problems and discussion. He also did much of the testing of the therapist and verbalized most of the hostile feelings toward authority figures. James on the other hand, as is suggested above, is most therapist-oriented. His moralisms set him up as group superego and through the interplay of his attitudes with those of the others, both sides of the conflict situation in which all are involved were presented. The spontaneous response to each other's comments rather than waiting for the therapist's mediation seem to signal important communication of these conflicting attitudes. James role has not yet clearly emerged.

In general, the group has adopted early analytic attitudes and seems willing, despite the presence of the observer, to verbalize feelings.

Tony's spontaneity may be a clue to this and that such progress may continue as the group develops.

Summary of Meeting No. 6—RG II: This meeting highlighted the implications of a group setting in which the highly structured characteristics of a Remedial Reading situation and the relatively unstructured characteristics of psychotherapy are rapidly and flexibly interchangeable. In this group there were rapidly fluctuating but quantitatively small peaks of tension because of the ease with which a member who found the therapeutic situation uncomfortable was able to request a shift to the reading situation. Thus at this early stage of the group no one was unduly threatened; the therapist was able to perceive the present limits and areas of concern of each member and several areas of concern were tapped albeit where they might not have been under conditions of prolonged concentration. On one therapeutic problem the latter circumstances frequently result in limitations of time and shocks to other members resulting in their problems not being introduced. (In this situation George's concern about embarrassment and fear, Don's sexual concern, and Tony's insecurity about girls, with whatever element might have linked them were all introduced.)

This leaves the possibility open for the continuation of such "hit and run" methods to the exclusion of prolonged and potentially effective therapy. However, as long as the therapist continues to have some control over the minute to minute content of the meeting, this is unlikely. There is the accompanying advantage of gradual de-traumatizing of much material that might otherwise be frightening.

This meeting featured Tony's and Don's efforts at task orientation. (Don's effort was unclear and may well be an effort to manipulate the therapist.) The meeting also included George's compulsive rushes into significant material and then out again and his relative intolerance of the task-oriented activity of the others, as well as his anxiety during periods when he was not in group focus. As a result a kind of balanced oscillation was achieved with alternations from problem solving to avoid operations.

It is of significance to note that there is a great deal of interpersonal comment and exchange between the members and there is a feeling of what Redl has called "groupiness."

RG III—Interview Group Therapy

Summary of Meeting No. 1— *RG III*: This meeting featured many silences as the therapist attempted to bring the group quickly into a realization of the treatment goals of the meetings. As a result, the members resisted the rapid forward movement by failing to give relevant material as requested by the therapist early in the meeting. Therapist was then faced with the problem of whether to interpret silences, to merely facilitate further discussion after the silence or to allow the silences to persist. He usually employed the second method thus giving the group a chance to think about the disturbing question although they did not reply to it. This also permitted the group to become somewhat dependent upon the therapist, a potentially useful situation at this stage of group treatment.

As the meeting continued, it seemed that certain members (Robert, Dick and Jim), became increasingly voluble. This was facilitated by Dick's impulsiveness and willingness to deal with sensitive matters.

The group's initial resistance to the therapist's effort to

bring them out served as a means of protecting themselves from a clear perception of what their job was in group treatment. Toward the end of the meeting, as they became more comfortable, their interest in "What we are doing here" became more pronounced and organized. There was little group interaction in the meeting. The only suggestion of it arose out of some smiles when Tony said he had never been "scared." Also Dick's attempts to relate humorously with the others was generally rebuffed by their sobriety.

In general, the meeting might be characterized as lacking in spontaneity and by a somewhat directive role of the therapist. It is of interest here that none of the boys brought up the problem of reading, although all have reading difficulties.

Summary of Meeting No. 2—RG III: Tension and resistance were extremely high during this meeting. The group has apparently become concerned over why they are here and a little puzzled by the new evident expectation of the therapist. There was a determined effort to find an answer to this problem by passively insisting that the therapist supply structure for the group (that he take the lead). This may also have been a passive resistance to the therapists' intrusions into their private worlds. (The therapist requested several times that they "tell what goes through your mind.") The potential source of difficulty may have been their expectation that what was demanded was a restitution of the "bad things" that they had done or thought of and this is in sharp conflict with their desire to conform to the therapists' demands and leadership.

The role of Dick in the group has devolped into a key one as the most impulsive. Individually he has helped the others say some of the things that disturb them, yet he also helps to keep tension high by verbalizing the suppressed and perhaps repressed feelings of several of them.

The level of involvement was another variable that

seemed to be moderately high at the beginning of the meeting and fell rapidly as the tension rose. This too would be consistent with the hypothesis that with low cohesiveness (as in the early stages of the group where the value of the group or attachment to it has not devolepd) a rise in tension will result in centrifugal pressure on the group rather than forcing it into some other type of operation such as aggressiveness or problem solving, etc.

Summary of Meeting No. 6—RG III: This meeting revolved in large part about several disturbing features. One, the observer with whom they were intensely concerned for the first 10 to 15 minutes of the meeting; two, Dick, who provided a constant disturbance throughout the meeting; and three, the intrusion of three strangers, one of them a policeman, who entered momentarily for various reasons. The disturbance arising from the group's concern over the role of the observer was dispelled very quickly after Dick clarified the nature of the concern by announcing "He writes everything we say." While Dick's activity was generally quite useful at the moment, his later activity had several other implications. It was a little annoying to Robert and Tony who regarded it simply as "crazy." However it simultaneously offered them a way of avoiding disturbing discussion and an object of interest to focus on other than their own problems or discomfort. It may also be instrumental in uniting other group members in the task of "changing the psychological group" so as to extrude the series of disturbances in the form of controlling an extremely deviate member. Whether this was a therapeutically useful kind of group cohesiveness remains to be seen. The therapist is now faced with the alternate problem of the effect on the group and on his own role of intervening to control Dick at this time. We also note the possibility that Dick's activity may either interfere with or hasten the development of a therapeutic goal orientation in the group. In the latter case, it would probably arise as a result of a field situation in which a disliked person posed a barrier to the achievement of what was at the moment an indifferent goal. The failings of the goal might then increase measurably.

It is difficult to discuss group tension in this meeting. It was disrupted as rapidly as it emerged by Dick's antics although at another level a gradual dissatisfaction with his role was emerging. There were several peaks of potential conflict resulting largely from Dick's baiting of the therapist and several moments when the group seemed to anticipate the therapists' administration of the reprimand that Dick seemed to be testing for. By and large the therapist remained permissive and tolerant of Dick's antics, thus not submitting to what may be described as manipulation by the patient. It is difficult at this time to assess the effects of this program by the therapist on group mores and processes.

CHAPTER V

DISCUSSION

Introduction

THE GENERAL APPROACH to clients and the selection of treatment techniques are influenced by the particular function of a social agency. When the treatment of delinquency is the special function, the agencies' procedures will differ from those applied in an agency with a nondelinquent case load, even though the basic treatment method and the underlying psychological assumptions are much the same in both settings. In a children's court clinic, for example, where there is a high concentration of a certain type of pathology, a particular kind of therapeutic approach is indicated. With few exceptions, the adolescents referred to the clinic are expressing their difficulties in acting-out behavior, with its accompanying hostility to persons in authority. They reach the clinic via the court and this fact alone induces negative attitudes that must be handled at the outset of treatment.

If treatment is to be appropriate to the delinquent's particular needs, it must be a flexible process continuously modified to meet the change in his social situation and in his feelings. His responses to the treatment situation can have little meaning unless they are viewed within the framework of the many significant and often overwhelming experiences with which he must cope in his daily living. Although no competent therapist treats his patient in a vacuum, the one who is working with delinquents must be particularly careful to avoid this error. No treatment process is really useful unless it takes into consideration the pressing reality conditions that form the context of the client's life. With the delinquent, this context would seem to be clearly evident and difficult to ignore, in view of the kinds of pressure from the court, school, family and neighbors to which he is often subjected. Peck and Bellsmith have stated that treatment should be conceived as "an attempt to provide adolescents and their families with a living experience that takes into account who the client is, the nature of his world, and his particular needs, problems, and strengths" (87, p. 21).

The present study was an attempt to evaluate a form of treatment that was, so to speak, "tailor made" for a specific group of delinquent children: those who manifest a reading disability in conjunction with severe emotional disturbance. The problem, as stated (p. 1), was to investigate the effectiveness of tutorial group therapy in facilitating psycho-social adjustment and correcting some aspects of reading retardation.

The two major hypotheses proposed in this study were as follows: 1) that tutorial group therapy will be more effective than group remedial reading or interview group therapy in improving psycho-social adjustment, and 2) that tutorial group therapy will be more effective than group remedial reading or interview group therapy in improving reading.

Improvement in Reading

The degree of improvement in reading in each of the three experimental groups was presented and analyzed in the preceding chapter. While the figures in the foregoing tables (Tables X-XIII) speak for themselves, it may be valuable to highlight and discuss the differences between the groups.

If we take first the group which received tutorial therapy (RG II) and compare it with the remedial reading group, we find no statistically significant differences in regard to reading improvement. It is noted, however, that the tutorial therapy group (RG II) showed a mean reading gain of 1.8 grades, while the remedial reading group (RG I) manifested a gain of 1.1 grades in reading. When the means gains in reading were converted into percentages, the tutorial therapy group showed a 35% greater improvement than the remedial reading group.

Passing now to a consideration of the difference between the tutorial therapy group and the interview therapy group the following may be noted. The tutorial therapy group showed a mean reading gain of 1.8 grades as compared to the mean gain of .7 grades for the interview therapy group. In terms of percentage gain, the tutorial therapy group manifested a 48% greater gain than the interview therapy group. In both comparisons these results, however, were not statistically significant.

There are several points of interest in the above-mentioned results: 1) each of the three groups showed an improvement in reading; 2) the tutorial therapy group showed a tendency toward greater improvement in reading than either of the other two experimental groups, and 3) the interview therapy group manifested the least improvement in reading.

It can be expected that children with marked reading disabilities who receive no treatment of any sort, will show little or no improvement in their reading. Hildreth (55) indicates that disabled readers are essentially unable to improve through their own efforts. Blair (17) with the same point of view, states that giving no attention to the reading disability will result in no improvement and possibly great-er retardation. Betts (11) and Harris (51) report somewhat categorically that children with reading disabilities do not improve without treatment.

In light of the above, it is of note that the group which received psychotherapy, but no remedial attention (RG III), showed an improvement of .7 grades in reading at the close of the experimental period. This finding tends to support Gann's hypothesis that "Helping to build emotional security may be essential in stimulating greater participation and better achievement (in reading)." The finding of reading improvement in the interview therapy group is also consistent with the results of earlier studies described in Chapter II. Axline, Bills and McGann have reported that psychotherapy with retarded readers tend to improve their reading.

While the results of the present study indicate that group psychotherapy improved the reading of retarded readers, they also reveal that: greater improvement in reading was achieved by group remedial reading and that the greatest improvement in reading occurred in the tutorial therapy group where there was an integration of remedial and thera-peutic techniques.

Fisher (36) in reporting on a study quite similar in de-sign to the present investigation, indicates that the greatest improvement in reading was achieved by the group which received group therapy with no remedial reading. He re-ports also, that the group which received remedial reading with no psychotherapy showed the least improvement in reading. Fisher's findings differ markedly from the results of the present investigation which indicated that the least improvement in reading was achieved by the group which received group therapy with no remedial reading.

The above differences may be due to a significant difference in the designs of the two studies. In Fisher's study, a remedial teacher and a psychotherapist were involved in the conducting of the experimental groups. Thus, the personality of the group leader was an uncontrolled factor. One might speculate that his findings are as much a result of the personalities of the group leaders as of the techniques that were utilized. In the present study, the investigator conducted all three groups, thereby controlling the personality variable.

In Fisher's investigation, a third group received group therapy and remedial reading. The therapy and remedial reading were conducted in separate sessions and by different leaders. Thus this particular group was exposed to two different "personalities": One a teacher and the other a therapist. Fisher reports that this third group showed a greater reading improvement than the "pure" remedial group but a lesser improvement than that "pure" therapy group. In discussing his results, Fisher suggests that negative attitudes toward remedial reading and the remedial teacher impeded the progress in the group which received remedial reading and group therapy.

The present investigation showed that the group which combined remedial reading and psychotherapy (RG II) manifested the greatest improvement in reading. On the basis of Fisher's findings and the results of the present study, one might agree that it is as unrealistic (and damaging) for a therapist to ignore the reading problems of his patient, as it is for a remedial teacher to ignore the emotional problems of her student. Dreikurs states:

> Corrective measures should not be limited to the area of deficiency, but should be applied to the larger issues and the psychological dynamics underlying this deficiency. The teacher cannot ignore the faulty values of the child, his mistaken self concepts and erroneous approaches.

Efforts to change them should become the essence of remedial teacher (30, p. 4).

The results of the present study suggest that we cannot consider the reading problems of a child apart from his total functioning as an individual. Effective remedial treatment appears to necessitate a modified psychotherapeutic approach incorporating treatment techniques designed to deal with the child's unproductive attitudes and emotional conflicts and remedial techniques designed to yield those positive educational experiences which lead to a more satisfactory orientation toward reading.

Improvement in Psycho-Social Adjustment

In all of the measures of psycho-social adjustment used in this study, the group which received tutorial therapy showed greater improvement than either of the other two experimental groups. In the sections that follow, the differences between the groups will be highlighted and discussed.

Davidson Rorschach Signs

In comparing the three groups we find that RG II (tutorial group therapy) manifests a 45% greater improvement in adjustment than RG I (group remedial reading) and a 13% improvement than RG III (interview group therapy). These results when subjected to an analysis of variance, were found to be significant at the 5% level of confidence. Further analysis of the data revealed that RG II's superiority over RG I was significant at the 5% level of confidence. The superiority of RG II over RG III was found to be not statistically significant. As expected, RG III's superiority to RGI was found to be statiscally signficant (5% level).

The above findings highlight the effectiveness of tutorial group therapy in bringing about positive changes in what may be referred to as "inner adjustment."

Haggerty-Olson-Wickman Behavior Rating Scale Schedule B

The H.O.W. Behavior Rating Scale, Schedule B, consists of a graphic rating scale for each of 35 intellectual, physical, social and emotional traits. By use of the H.O.W. the behavior status of a problem child may be designated in quantitative terms. The scale seems particularly appropriate for use in the present study in that it allows for ratings in five areas of adjustment: intellectual, physical, social, emotional and total. Each subject was rated on the basis of his group behavior in the initial five sessions ("pre") and in the last five sessions, ("post"). The ratings were made by the psychologist who functioned as an observer in all group sessions.

If we take first the area of intellectual adjustment, we find that RG II made a 33% greater improvement than RG I and a 17% greater gain than RG III. The superiority of RG II over either of the other two groups, was found to be significant at the 1% level of confidence. Of note is the finding that RG III did significantly better (5% level) than RG I in this particular area of adjustment.

While each of the groups show some positive change in the area of physical adjustment, the differences between the groups are not statistically significant. Worthy of mention is the tendency toward greater change again evidenced in RG II (tutorial group therapy). RG II made a 10% greater gain in physical adjustment than RG I, and an 11% greater improvement than RG III.

Passing now to the area of social adjustment it is noted that RG II made a 19% greater gain than RG I and a 21% greater improvement than RG III. The superiority of RG II over the other two groups was found to be significant at the 5% level of confidence. It is somewhat surprising to note that the remedial reading group and the interview

therapy group do not differ significantly in terms of improved social adjustment.

In terms of emotional adjustment, the groups again show
marked differences, with RG II manifesting rather clear
cut superiority. In this area, RG II made a 23% greater gain
than RG III and a 21% greater gain than RG I. These findings are significant at the 1% level of confidence.

As might be expected from the preceding data, RG II
(tutorial group therapy) made significantly greater improvement in total adjustment than either group remedial
reading (RG I) or interview group therapy (RG III). The
over-all gain in adjustment for RG II was 35% as compared
to gains of 15% for RG III and 10% for RG I. In comparing the differences between the groups, it was found that
RG II's superiority over RG I was significant at the 1%
level and that RG II's superiority over RG III was significant at the 5% level of confidence. Noteworthy is the finding of no significant difference between group remedial
reading and interview group therapy in terms of over-all
gain in adjustment.

In summary, then, certain trends emerge from the
H.O.W. "pre" and "post" data: 1) tutorial group therapy
consistently evidenced superior improvement in adjustment when compared to group remedial reading and interview group therapy, and 2) group remedial reading kept
pace with interview group therapy in the reduction of maladjustment.

Psychologists' Ratings

The "pre" and "post" Summary Charts of Test Findings
of each of the 21 subjects were independently inspected and
rated by three judges. The Summary Chart of Test Findings
has been described in an earlier section (Chapter IV).
As was previously indicated the judges rates each subject

on a four-point scale of improvement for six personality areas. The reliability of the ratings is established by the finding of 90.50% agreement among the judges. In view of the high reliability it was decided to average the ratings of the three judges in order to facilitate intergroup comparisons.

The average total score for each subject was used as an index of over-all change and these data were examined statistically. On the basis of the judges' ratings RG II (tutorial group therapy) was found to have made significantly greater improvement in over-all change than either RG I (group remedial reading) or RG III (interview group therapy). These findings were significant at the 1% level of confidence. Again it should be noted that the differences between group remedial reading and interview group therapy were found to be not statistically significant.

A word about the qualitative findings in comparing the three groups on six personality continua. RG II consistently showed greater improvement in all personality areas than either RG I or RG III. A composite summary of the qualitative differences between the three groups indicates the following: RG II was slightly superior to RG III in terms of increased productivity and markedly superior to RG I. Whereas both RG II and RG III showed considerable positive change in test productivity, RG I showed no change.

As might be expected, RG II's responses were less stereotyped and more original. There were no noticeable changes on the thought content continuum for either RG I or RG III.

Apparently related to the factor of Rorschach responsiveness, is that of available constructive fantasy. Eighty-six per cent of the subjects in RG II were rated as showing "partial improvement" in available constructive fantasy, whereas only 29% of RG III and 0% of RG I were so rated.

Another area which differentiates between the groups and reflects RG II's superiority is that of relation to reality. The remedial reading group evidenced no change in this area. Both therapy groups (RG II and RG III) manifested considerable positive change in this respect with RG II showing a 28% greater improvement than RG III.

In the area of improved emotional tone, the groups are again sharply dissimilar. RG II evidences a 28% greater improvement than RG III and a 43% greater improvement than RG I. In essence, the "post" test protocols of RG II reflect less repression and inner conflict and greater capacity for constructive emotional expression. The majority of the "post" protocols in RG I and RG III reveal continued inner conflict over the expression of affect.

The passivity-aggression continuum also seems to differentiate between the groups. Here again RG II evidences the greatest improvement. In RG II, 86% of the subjects were improved as compared to 29% in RG I and 0% in RG III.

In summary, then, the subjects in tutorial group therapy (RG II) evidenced greater test productivity, less inner conflict, greater spontaneity of affect and an accompanying increase in available constructive fantasy. Relation with reality is considerably improved and this appears to be related to their evidently greater ability to control the acting out of aggressive impulses.

The remedial reading group (RG I) evidences little qualitative change in their test protocols. Except for slight improvement in the areas of passivity-aggression and emotional tone their "post" protocols are essentially similar to their "pre" records.

And lastly, the interview therapy group (RG III) seems to fall midway between the two extremes: they showed a trend to greater improvement than RG I but not as great as RG II. In general, the subjects in interview group therapy showed somewhat greater productivity, increased reality contact, and a tendency toward less inner conflict.

It appears from the above that the psychologists' ratings tend to support the previously mentioned findings (Davidson Scale and H.O.W. Behavior Rating Scale) that RG II effected significantly greater improvement in psycho-social adjustment than either of the two other experimental groups.

Social Workers' Ratings

The social workers judgments indicated that RG II (tutorial group therapy) effected greater improvement in psycho-social adjustment than either RG I (group remedial reading) or RG III (interview group therapy). It is to be noted, however, that the differences among the groups were not statistically significant.

As previously indicated, two psychiatric social workers evaluated the case material of each subject at the conclusion of the experimental period. Apparent changes in interpersonal relationships and attitudes and behavior were noted. The social workers' evaluations were based on the following material which was available for each child: probation officer's investigation, school reports, and "pre" and "post" social worker interviews with child and parents. The social workers' evaluations were based on clinical judgment of trend and not on formal criteria.

In comparing the groups, certain qualitative trends are apparent. All of the groups show improvement in each of the ten adjustment areas considered, with RG II showing a consistent trend toward superiority. In most of the adjustment areas there is little difference between the groups in terms of degree of improvement. Several areas, however, do show major group differences.

Let us first consider school adjustment. In this area RG

II shows a 28% greater improvement than RG I and a 43% greater improvement than RG III. It is of interest to note that the trend toward better school adjustment as evidenced by the respective rankings of the three groups (II, I, III) corresponds with the trend toward greater gain in reading evidenced by the same rank order (II, I, III). Thus the tutorial therapy group, which manifested the greatest gain in reading also shows a trend toward greater gain in school adjustment. In terms of the relative standing of all three groups it is evident that the interview therapy group (RG III) which received no remedial assistance showed the least improvement in school adjustment. It may be that greater ability to read resulted in a more positive orientation to school. We might further speculate that the treatment relationships with the therapist (who was viewed in both RG I and RG II as a teacher), resulted in a somewhat different perception of teachers in general. We shall come back to this point in a later section of the discussion.

Another area which seems to show marked group differences is that of legal adjustment. Here the subjects were evaluated purely in terms of the continuance or discontinuance of antisocial behavior. In RG II and RG III, 71% of the subjects were rated as improved. In RG I 57% were rated as improved. While 14% of the subjects in RGI were rated as "worse" none of the subjects in either RG II or RG III were so rated.

In view of the reduction of antisocial behavior indicated above, we would expect that these groups would reflect better relationships with authority. While each group did show improvement in adjustment to authority, the tutorial therapy group made the greatest gains in this area. The social workers' data indicates that 86% of RG II were rated improved. Of this 86%, 43% received the rating "considerable improvement."

In many of the behavorial areas evaluated by the social workers, there was little difference among groups. The findings may be summarized as follows: RG II was found to have made the greatest improvement in all areas evaluated; RG I did better than RG III in terms of school adjustment; RG III did better than RG I in terms of community adjustment. As indicated earlier, these results were not significant when subjected to an analysis of variance.

The Therapeutic Process

Despite variations in technique and emphasis, most forms of group therapy (interview group therapy, group centered psycho-therapy, psychoanalytic group therapy, etc.) have similar basic principles which they share with individual treatment. All forms of therapy attempt to create a setting in which patients can have helpful new experiences and learn from them; the basic objective is to bring about corrective emotional experiences.

Neubauer states, "Therapy directs itself to the deviant aspects of personality, the symptoms of the character disturbance, with a view toward effecting change in individual pathology. Making use of a specific technique consciously applied it approaches conflicts in order to free the energies bound within them, thus making these energies available for healthy growth" (81, p. 316).

Education, on the other hand, directs itself to those functions of the ego undisturbed by conflict. It requires the ability to judge, to learn by experience, to gain understanding and to plan. While education and psychotherapy are basically dissimilar, an educational experience can and very often does have therapeutic effects. Witness the degree of improvement in psycho-social adjustment (Chapter IV) effected by group remedial reading. Similarly, a therapeutic experience can result in educational gains (note reading improvement in RG III).

While many authorities (81) view with scepticism the proposal that the approaches of education and therapy be combined, Neubauer has commented:

> While it may be possible and at the time even necessary to use education in a therapeutic situation, its specific application should arise from a clear understanding of the necessity or its employment. Otherwise, combinations of education and therapy may lead to dilutions and confusions. Specific techniques should be applied for specific purposes (81, p. 316).

In the present experiment, psychotherapy and remedial reading were planfully integrated in the form of tutorial group therapy. The results indicate that tutorial group therapy is more effective than either group remedial reading or interview group therapy in treating delinquent children who present a reading disability in conjunction with emotional disturbance.

Although there is a good deal of overlap in the three group approaches utilized in the present investigation, there are several areas of difference that can be distinguished, especially in technique and philosophy.

First, it is assumed that in both therapy and teaching, there is the common goal of developing sufficient psychosocial growth in the child so that more effective functioning will be possible. In group remedial reading, the teacher-student relationship allows the educational process to help the child learn and grow, but it consistently remains oriented to the objectives of remedial reading, rather than therapy. The relationship between teacher and child, and between group and child is never interpreted in the group remedial setting. In tutorial group therapy, however, the therapist-child relationship, as well as the group-child relationship, is often interpreted.

Second, in the remedial setting, the teacher attempts to

help the child with the reality pressures which have increased his need for disturbed behavior. In teaching (remedial reading) there is the opportunity to increase the child's self esteem and ego strength, by convincing him that he can learn and control his learning; whereas in psychotherapy, an attempt is made to free the child of his own internationalized needs for disturbed behavior by affording him verbal or experiential insight into the ways in which he handles conflict. In tutorial group therapy both approaches are utilized to mutual advantage. The members of the tutorial group are encouraged to express their feelings about reading, school, and learning process and the teacher-therapist. The remedial aspects of the tutorial therapy group stimulate significant attitudes and emotions in the child and provide the therapist with material that can make the group process a more meaningful experience for the child, both educationally and therapeutically.

Third, the remedial teacher focuses on the "situational present," whereas the therapist focuses on the "historical present." In tutorial group therapy, the emphasis is on the "historical present" specifically as it relates to the learning process.

Fourth, as can be seen from much of the above, the remedial teacher deals with the child's learning problems through the use of reality, rather than through the interpretation of it as in the case of therapy. In tutorial group therapy, however, the therapist both uses and interprets reality in accordance with the specific group needs at any particular period of the group's development. This flexibility in technique is viewed as crucial to the success of tutorial therapy.

Having thus described some of the basic differences between the three experimental groups evaluated in the present investigation, let us now take a closer look at the actual process and content of the tutorial therapy group.

A. Tutorial therapy is anchored in an area where the delinquent child is aware of, or can be made aware of, his inadequacy, and "see" the possibility of concrete help. The therapeutic relationship is established on the basis of tangible help and only after the relationship is established do we attempt to redirect aggressive behavior.

B. The tutorial therapy group is reality oriented in that it resembles the classroom situation; the members consistently referred to the therapist as "teacher" and one member commented at an early meeting, "It's like school, but better." The therapist explicitly states that he is primarily interested in that which prevented them from learning to read rather than in teaching them to read. Because of the therapist's attitude and orientation, he was perceived as a "different type of teacher": one who was not interested in achievement, per se, but rather in how lack of achievement effected the adolescent in his everyday life.

C. The therapeutic atmosphere is permissive and accepting. The child feels free to do as he wished; he need not achieve to be accepted, he need not "want" to learn to read.

When Al, a sullen and resistive youngster, expressed considerable discouragement and implied that school could not give him the material rewards that he desired, the therapist did not dispute this, but expressed a warm understanding of Al's concern about making good. Al required further evidence of the therapist's attitude. First he asked whether he could continue in the group if he left school, and was reassured that he could. Immediately thereafter he asked whether he could come to the group if he went back to school and learned to read there. The therapist explained that he was welcome no matter what he did. (Observer's recording.)

D. The dual orientation of the group, namely, that they can "work on reading" or "talk," permits easy movement from one activity to another and thereby highlights reactions to stress and patterns of resistance. This provides the therapist the opportunity to maintain therapeutically optimal levels of tension and to constructively utilize and/or interpret resistance. In the early meetings, at a point where group discussion of personal problems aroused a considerable degree of anxiety, someone would suggest that we "cut the talk and get back to reading." And conversely, at times when the remedial work became frustrating and "boring" there would be pressure from one member or another to discuss some personal "non-reading" problem. During the early sessions of the group treatment, the therapist would accede to the group wishes without comment or intervention. As the meetings progressed, the therapist became more active and began to point out that there was some pattern to the groups activities, and to interpret resistances.

During a reading exercise, Jack rationalized an error by stating that he was "nervous." When the therapist questioned him about what might make him nervous, the following ensued:

Jack: I'm afraid I'm making a mistake.
Therapist: Why should you be afraid of that?
Jack: You get ashamed and embarrassed.
Therapist: Is that how you feel?
Jack: Let's get back to the reading.
Therapist: I guess you'd rather read than talk about being embarrassed.

(The above was followed by a rather extensive discussion of embarrassment and defenses against it.) (Observer's recording.)

E. A technique utilized with great success in the tutorial group was that of the spontaneous story. This technique is in some ways similar to the dramatic dialogue technique reported by McGann (72). The spontaneous story, as employed in this investigation, is the invention of the entire group. In this way, the group story incorporates the fantasies of almost all the group members and provides the therapist with a medium of operation. The implications of the story for the child and group are often far reaching and the therapeutic task appears to lie not only in bringing about the invention of the story and the production of fantasies, but also in the handling of material that grows out of the story. The material once obtained, is typed and used as reading material in subsequent sessions. Although very often the stories were written on a level above that at which they were capable of reading, their interest in and familiarity with the content, increased their motivation to learn to read their own stories. It is of interest to note that they were often more successful in reading this material than in reading standard stories at their appropriate grade levels.

Following are examples of stories produced during the group sessions:

"She's in Danger"

This is Mary. She's a bad lady. She's bad because of her mind. She has bad ideas. She has ideas of stealing money and killing people and murdering rich people. She smokes reefers. And she smokes cigars. About 24 years old. She's not married but she has about 9 kids. She burns her kids. She's Japanese. She wants everything her way and gets everything she wants. She wants money and gold and all those things. She won't last long. She'll either die or be sent to jail.

"Beware of Scarface"

Scarface is 21 years old and single. He sticks up banks. He's the leader of a gang. He's also king of the gamblers. He's a rough guy. He looks rough and he acts rough. He was treated rough when he was a kid and became rough. His parents treated him rough. He never got anything from his parents. He had to rob. His parents died when he was little. Some man picked him out of the street and put him in a home. He escaped. Later on he had a fight with a cop and got a scar. Since then he had a grudge against cops.

He was good until he got scarred. He had some bad breaks with girls and things like that. Ever since he got his scar things went bad and so he became bad.

After he robs a bank so many times he feels sorry for himself and gets shot and the cops catch them all.

"Eddie Soda Pop"

One day Eddie Soda Pop came to court. He came to court because he was caught robbing a large sum of money. He came to court with his mother and father and the witness and the guy that was robbed. He felt embarrassed and was afraid he was going to be sent away. He told the Judge he was framed. The Judge said he was guilty. He asked for his story. He said to Eddie, why did you take the money? Eddie said, I had a chance to take the money so I couldn't refuse. He said he bought a lot of clothes and took his girl out and later he got caught. He made his mother happy by buying her new things. He spent money at the races and lost.

I hereby sentence you to 5-10 years in Warwick. Eddie Soda Pop says I want to see my lawyer. Judge says, too late, case closed. So that ends the story of Eddie Soda Pop.

He goes to prison. The name of the prison was Princeton. He was a wise guy so he was sent to the hole. He stayed there for a few weeks and came out seeing black. Sent him to hospital in prison—he was too skinny. In the hospital he died. He died of starvation.

They transferred him to nut house—he was cracking up. They put him in a room by himself. He was a kleptomaniac. He just robs for pleasure. He breaks away. He's a nut and tells the Soda Pop people he owns the place. They tell him he's nuts and he says I know it. They send him to Wards Island and he gets the chair for killing someone. They burn him and put his ashes in a soda pop bottle. He came to life again. They bury the soda pop bottle with a big funeral and a little soda pop bottle is a big casket.

F. As identification with the therapist is developed, there is an increasing adoption of his attitudes, values and goals. The peer group, known to be of fundamental importance in the development of attitudes, facilitates this process through its subtle pressures to conformity. Thus, during a discussion of attitudes toward reading:

> Al demonstrated his ambivalence by insisting desperately that he did not want to learn to read. However, Tony and Jack expressed strong desires to learn to read and spell. Both stressed to Al the difficulties he would encounter by not being able to read. After a period of silence, Al stated that he would go along with the group in order to see "whether there was anything to this reading business." (Observer's recording.)

The foregoing has described some of the significant aspects of content and process in tutorial group therapy. Before concluding this discussion, a word about the individual members of the tutorial group. In the course of treatment the therapeutic relationship varied considerably from child to child, not only in terms of the frequency of contact between therapist and child in any one meeting, but also in terms of the quality and intensity of the relationship. Some children resisted contact for long periods of time. With others there was a tendency to become overinvolved in a demanding and manipulative manner. For many the significance of their relationship with the therapist and group could only be ascertained over a long period of time, for they showed varying degrees of involvement in the group's activities and discussions. The differences in relationships are suggestive of the fact that different children use the therapist and the group situation in unique fashions.

Not only do different children appear to make individualized and unique use of the therapeutic situation, but it also seems that different children start therapy from different points. In would appear to follow, theoretically at least, that different children may have different optimal periods of therapeutic termination. In terms of the over-all results of this study, it may be that the therapeutic experience was continued long enough for some of the children to show demonstrable results, but not for others. It is to be noted again, however, that the tutorial therapy group consistently evidenced superiority to group remedial reading and interview group therapy on all of the evaluative measures used in this investigation.

CHAPTER VI

CONCLUSIONS, IMPLICATIONS AND
SUGGESTIONS FOR FURTHER RESEARCH

Introduction

T HE PURPOSE of this study, as originally stated (Chapter I), was to investigate the effectiveness of tutorial group therapy in facilitating pscho-social adjustment and correcting some aspects of reading retardation. The stated hypotheses (Chapter I) were as follows:

That tutorial group therapy will improve psycho-social adjustment and that the tutorial group therapy subjects will show greater improvement in adjustment than the members in either of the other two groups.

That tutorial group therapy will improve reading ability and that the tutorial group therapy subjects will show greater improvement in reading than the members in either of the other two groups.

Conclusions

The results of the present investigation seem to warrant the following conclusions:

1. Tutorial group therapy affected greater improvement in psycho-social adjustment than either group remedial reading or interview group therapy.

   a. The superiority of tutorial group therapy was found to be statistically significant on the following measures of adjustment: Davidson Rorschach Signs; Intellectual, Social, Emotional and Total adjustment scales of the H.O.W. Behavior Rating Scale, Schedule B, and the psychologist's rating of adjustment change based on a battery of projective tests.

b. The tutorial therapy group showed a greater tendency toward improvement (though not statistically significant) than did group remedial reading or interview group therapy on the following measures of adjustment: Physical Adjustment Scale of the H.O.W. Behavior Rating Scale, Schedule B, and the social workers' ratings of improvement in adjustment.

2. Tutorial group therapy resulted in improved reading ability and the tutorial therapy group showed a greater tendency toward improvement (though not statistically significant) than did the remedial reading group or the interview therapy group.

3. The greatest positive change in psycho-social adjustment and the greatest improvement in reading took place in the group which received tutorial group therapy.

Implications

To determine the wide implications of the results of this study, it is necessary to determine the extent to which the 21 subjects included in the study are representative of the entire population of delinquent children and of non-delinquent children with reading disabilities.

Gann, Siegel and others have shown that children with reading disabilities exhibited as great a variety of emotional problems as could be found in populations of emotionally disturbed children who had no reading disabilities. No common personality patterns were found in populations of retarded readers that could distinguish them from good readers.

Traxler has indicated that approximately 10% of the

national school population requires special help because of retardation in reading. An unpublished survey by the writer in 1951 revealed that 84% of the children active in the treatment clinic of New York City Children's Court manifested a reading retardation of 2 or more years. Harrower (54) reporting on a study of 225 juvenile first offenders indicates that 76% of the children were retarded by 2 or more years, and that over half of the retarded 76% manifested a disability of 5 or more years.

It is felt that the retarded readers in a delinquent population exhibit as varied a group of emotional problem as might be seen in the nondelinquent population of retarded readers. The basic distinction between the experimental population of retarded readers and the general population of retarded readers appears to lie in the experimental population's history of severe social and emotional deprivation, accompanied by antisocial aggressive behavior. In addition, it may be that there is a greater degree of emotional disturbance in a delinquent retarded reader population than in a non-delinquent retarded reader population.

The purpose of this study was the evaluation of a new form of treatment, primarily for use with a delinquent population of retarded readers. While the results of the study may in some ways be applicable to the general population of retarded readers, this discussion will be restricted to implications for the treatment of delinquent children.

Remedial Reading Is Not Enough

The results of this study support the philosophy and approach of the best modern pedagogical practices. Educators no longer stress the mechanical, isolated, teaching of reading. The emphasis is rather to delay the teaching of reading until such time as the child is ready and mature enough emotionally and physically to not only master the technical aspects of reading, but to comprehend and enjoy reading experiences. In this way, each child is encouraged to proceed at his own rate and to develop according to his own capacity. These being the goals, the modern teacher is concerned with the attitudes, interests and emotional adjustment of her students. The teacher is expected to be aware of group process and to use the group as a positive force in the development of the individual child. To a great extent, one might say that the modern remedial teacher uses her teaching skills in a therapeutic fashion.

While such a positive remedial program may be quite successful with nondelinquent children it has its shortcomings with delinquent children. Since learning is an ego function, the success of a remedial program depends on the cooperation of a "reasonable ego." Approaching the delinquent child with corrective measures which in many ways resemble his original traumatic experiences in reading (failure), may actually inhibit the process of remediation unless his emotional reactions to teacher and program are brought to the surface and handled therapeutically. In dealing with emotionally disturbed delinquent children, the best remedial program does not offer enough of a strategic change from the traumatic school situation to bring about such changes in their ego structure as to allow the development of a positive relationship with teacher and program. Without a positive teacher-student relationship, the best remedial program will be of limited value.

The results of this study indicate that the children who received group remedial reading improved their reading at a pace considerably slower than those who received tutorial group therapy and only slightly faster than those who received interview group therapy and no remedial reading. As far as improvement in adjustment is concerned, the children who received group remedial reading showed less positive change than the children in either of the other two experimental groups. Redl and Wineman, in discussing the problem of educating the emotionally disturbed delinquent child states the following:

> Good education is not enough for the cure of children who hate. Rather the reverse comes closer to the truth: in order for a good educational diet to take hold of these children at all, their basic ego disturbances must be repaired first (96, p. 242).

Psychotherapy Offers Too Little

Several investigators (5, 13, 36) have indicated that psychotherapy may be successfully employed in the treatment of reading disabilities. In the present study, the children who received interview group therapy improved in reading, but at a slower pace than those who received group remedial reading or tutorial group therapy. Thus, group psychotherapy appears to be less effective than either group remedial reading or tutorial group therapy in attempting to improve the reading ability of delinquent retarded readers. It appears, then, that therapy alone is not enough; or, that it has limited value when used as a substitute for a remedial program with delinquent children.

If psychotherapy alone, is not effective enough in terms of improving the reading ability of retarded delinquent children, what does it offer in the way of improved psychosocial adjustment? Here, too, the results of the present study tend to support the findings of Redl and Wineman:

> . . . are clearly beyond the resources of the interviewer or interview situations to cope with, and, inevitably force the therapist into acts of interference long before a transference neurosis or relationship can be established. Most importantly, too, the separation between the therapist's role and the rest of their lives constitute a tremendous advantage to their defenses against change (97, p. 21).

In the present study, the interview therapy group showed less of an improvement in psycho-social adjustment than did the tutorial therapy group. Beck (6) has stated that conventional therapeutic approaches are inappropriate for delinquent children. He indicates that what appears to be effective and appropriate is the type of program in which a therapeutic relationship:

> . . . is established on the basis of tangible help, and only after the relationship do we attempt to redirect the aggression (6, p. 5).

Tutorial group therapy appears to effectively overcome many of the obstacles in the treatment of delinquent children with reading disabilities. The techniques of tutorial therapy are the means and not the end—the means by which a positive therapeutic relationship is established with the child and group. A relationship which enables the child to learn and grow.

Remedial reading teachers and clinicians should therefore be trained in the principles and techniques of psychotherapy. Wherever possible, children with reading disabilities should be referred to competent psychotherapists who have had specialized training in the area of remedial reading.

Although this study has considerable interest in terms of remedial education it is perhaps more significant in its implications for the over-all approach to the treatment of the delinquent.

Some of the implications are self evident. Treatment in a group for many of these individuals is most productive when it begins by engaging them in some collaborative endeavor around matters that are concrete, of real and current concern, not too threatening yet linked to critical disturbances in nondelinquent life areas. Tutorial Group Therapy provides the kind of semi-structured situation which is more tolerable to most delinquent youngsters than the usual amorphous context of psychotherapy. It is true that the introduction of more structure into the therapeutic situation may be converted into a cover for the patient's resistance and for some patients this may be fatal. For most delinquents however, it is essential in that it provides an otherwise unattainable therapeutic opportunity.

Even when there are intra-psychic conflicts which seem to be closely related to remote happenings early in the individual's life, by the time he has "gotten into trouble" such disturbances may be discerned at many levels of functioning and in more than one lifearea. If, no matter how, the therapist is able to make meaningful contact within one of those areas, at some level where communication is possible, a therapeutic opportunity presents itself. To take advantage of such an opportunity one must be convinced that therapy can take place whenever the patient is planfully helped to alter some characteristic mode of operation related to his crucial life problems. When this occurs there is almost always a significant change in the intra-psychic structure.

There is no reason why the approach described in this study need be confined to the area of remedial education. We know that in play therapy it is not the precise nature of the play materials which determine the course of treatment but rather the way in which they are utilized in the service of communication and the extent to which they lend themselves to the expression of, and dealing with, the child's most pressing concerns. For those delinquents and pre-delinquents who see their current situation in terms of quitting school, finding a job, leaving home or improving their social performance one should be able to offer opportunities for participation in a group loosely structured around one or another of these matters. If the therapist is sufficiently flexible to both utilize the concerns to establish contact and employ them as a springboard he will then be able to provide a kind of dynamically oriented assistance which is centered about a crucial life area and thus achieve therapeutic objectives which might otherwise be unobtainable.

Such a suggestion implies neither a dilution of therapy nor the substituting of educational methods for therapeutic ones. It does not imply that teachers may be used instead of therapists or that group work agencies as they are presently constituted can replace clinics. It does, however, point to the need for moving some of our clinical personnel out of their relatively isolated physical settings and increasing the number attached to community institutions where they may be able to make more meaningful contacts with their prospective clients.

Certain of the suggestions made above also have some relevance to the much confused problem of prevention. Prevention, like treatment, must be linked to concrete services. In effective therapy these are provided with an awareness of both the strengths and the pathology of the individual recipient. In prevention we must delineate the epidemiological patterns in whole segments of the population and be ready to extend, alter, or create new services in a way which takes cognizance of the unmet needs of those deprived areas of our communities from which comes the greater part of the delinquent population.

BIBLIOGRAPHY

1. Abt, L. E., and Bellak, L.: *Projective Psychology*. New York, Knopf, 1950.
2. Addy, M. L.: Influence of personality traits on reading ability of eleven school children. *Educational Administration and Supervision, 32:555-558*, 1946.
3. Arthur, G.: *Tutoring as Therapy*. New York, Commonwealth Fund, 1946.
4. Axline, V. M.: *Play Therapy*. New York, Houghton, 1947.
5. Axline, V. M.: Nondirective therapy for poor readers. *J. Consulting Psychol., 2:61-69*, 1947.
6. Beck, B. M.: What we can do about juvenile delinquency. *Child Welfare, 33:3-7*, 1954.
7. Bell, J. E.: *Projective Techniques*. New York, Longmans, 1948.
8. Benjamin, J. D., and Ebaugh, F. G.: The diagnostic validity of the Rorschach Test. *Am. J. Psychiat., 94:*1163-1178, 1938.
9. Bennett, C. C.: *An Inquiry into the Genesis of Poor Readers*. Teachers College Contributions to Education, Number 755. New York, Columbia Univ. Press, 1935.
10. Bettelheim, B.: *Love Is Not Enough*. Glencoe, Illinois, Free Press, 1951.
11. Betts, E. A.: *The Prevention and Correction of Reading Disabilities*. New York, Row Peterson & Co., 1936.
12. Betts, E. A., and Betts, T. M.: *An Index to Professional Literature on Reading-Related Topics*. New York, Am. Bk. Co., 1945.

13. Bills, R. E.: Nondirective play therapy with retarded readers. *J. Consulting Psychol.*, *2:*140-149, 1950.
14. Bills, R. E.: Nondirective play therapy with well adjusted retarded readers. *J. Consulting Psychol.*, *4:*246-249, 1950.
15. Bird, G. E.: Personality factors in learning. *Personnel J.*, *6:*56-59, June, 1927.
16. Bixler, R. H.: Limits are therapy. *J. Consulting Psychol.*, *1:*1-11, 1949.
17. Blair, G. M.: *Diagnostic & Remedial Teaching in Secondary Schools.* New York, Macmillan, 1946.
18. Blanchard, P.: Psychogenic factors in some cases of reading disability. *Am. J. Orthopsychiat.*, *5:*361-371, 1935.
19. Blanchard, P.: Reading disability in relation to difficulties of personality and emotional development. *Ment. Hyg.*, *20:*384-413, 1936.
20. Blanchard, P. J.: Psychoanalytic contributions to the problems of reading disabilities. *Psychoanalyt. Study of the Child*, Vol. II, 1946.
21. Brown, J. F., and Rapaport, D.: The role of the psychologist in the psychiatric clinic. *Bull. Menninger Clin.*, *5:*75-84, 1941.
22. Campbell, D. T.: The indirect assessment of social attitudes. *Psychological Bull.*, *47:*15-38, 1950.
23. Challman, R. C.: Personality maladjustments and remedial reading. *J. Exceptional Child.*, *6:*7-11, 1939.
24. Cunningham, J. M.: Psychiatric case work as an epidemiological tool. *Am. J. Orthopsychiat.*, *18:*659, 1948.
25. Damereau, R.: Influence of treatment on the reading ability and behavior disorders of reading disability cases. *Smith College Studies in Social Work*, *5:*160-183, 1934.
26. Davidson, H. H.: A measure of adjustment obtained from the Rorschach Protocol. *J. Projective Techniques*, *14:*31-38, 1950.
27. Dearborn, W. F.: Structural factors which condition special disability in reading. *Proc. Am. A. Ment. Deficiency*, *38*, 1933.
28. Deri, S.: The Szondi Test. *Am. J. Orthopsychiat.*, *19:*447-

454, 1949.

29. Deri, S.: *Introduction to the Szondi Test.* New York, Grune & Stratton, 1949.

30. Dreikurs, R.: Emotional predispositions to reading difficulties. *NART News, II:4,* 1-4, October, 1952.

31. Eames, T. H.: A comparison of ocular characteristics of unselected and reading disability groups. *J. Educational Research, 25:211,* 1932.

32. Edwards, A. L.: *Experimental Design in Psychological Research.* New York, Rinehart, 1950.

33. Ephron, B. K.: *Emotional difficulties in Reading.* New York, Julian Press, 1953.

34. Fabian, A.: Reading disability—An index of pathology. *Presented at American Orthopsychiatric Association Conference,* 1954. Pending publication.

35. Fernald, G. M.: *Remedial Techniques in Basic School Subjects.* New York, McGraw-Hill, 1943.

36. Fisher, B.: *An Investigation of the Effectiveness of Group Therapy for the Remediation of Reading Disabilities.* Doctors Dissertation, School of Education, New York Univ., 1953.

37. Fisher, B.: A psychologist's evaluation of teachers' reports and suggestions for their improvement. *Educational Administration and supervision, 2:62-65,* 1953.

38. Fosberg, I. A.: An Experimental Study of the Reliability of the Rorschach Psychodiagnostic Technique. *Rorschach Research Exchange, 5:72-84,* 1941.

39. Frank, L. K.: *Projective Methods.* Springfield, Illinois, Charles C. Thomas, 1948.

40. Gann, E.: *Reading Difficulty and Personality Organization.* New York, King's, 1945.

41. Garrett, H. E.: *Statistics in Psychology and Education,* Third Edition. New York, Longmans, 1948.

42. Gates, A. I.: Frontiers in educational research in reading. *J. Educational Research, 40:338,* 1947.

43. Gates, A. I.: Failure in reading and social maladjustment. *J. Nat. Education A., 25:205-206,* 1936.

44. Gates, A. I.: *Gates Advanced Primary Reading Tests.* (Manual) New York, Columbia Univ., 1943.

45. Gates, A. I.: *The Improvement of Reading.* New York, Macmillan, 1947.

46. Goodenough, F. L., and Harris, D. B.: Studies in the psychology of children's drawings: II 1928-1949. *Psychological Bull.*, 369-433.

47. Gray, W. S.: *Gray Standardized Oral Reading Paragraphs.* Bloomington, Illinois, Public School Pub. Co., 1915.

48. Gunzberg, H. C.: The unsuccessful reader. *Ment. Health, London,* 8:34-37, 1948.

49. Haggerty, M. E., Olson, W. C., and Wickman, E. K.: *Haggerty-Olson-Wickman Behavior Rating Schedules.* New York, World Bk. Co., 1930.

50. Hardwick: Types of reading disability. *Childhood Education,* 8:425, 1932.

51. Harris, A. J.: *How to Increase Reading Ability.* New York, Longmans, 1948.

52. Harrower, M. R.: *Experimental Studies With the Szondi Test.* New York, Szondi Newsletter, 1953.

53. Harrower, M. R.: Visual aids in the presentation of test findings. *J. Projective Techniques,* 15:4-5, 1956.

54. Harrower, M. R.: Who Comes to Court? *Presented at the American Orthopsychiatric Conference,* 1954. Pending publication.

55. Hildreth, G.: *Learning the Three R's,* Second Edition. Philadelphia, Educational Publishers, 1947.

56. Hincks, E. M.: *Disability in Reading and Its Relation to Personality.* Harvard Monographs in Education, No. 7. Cambridge, Harvard, 1926.

57. Hinshelwood, J.: *Congenital Word-Blindness.* London, Lewis, 1917.

58. Hirsch, K.: Specific dyslexia or strephosymbolia. *Internat. J. Phoniatry,* 4, 1952.

59. Hunt, W. A., Klebanoff, S. G., Mensh, I. N., and Williams, M.: The validity of some abbreviated individual intelligence scales. *J. Consulting Psychol.,* 12:48-52, 1948.

60. Javal, Cited by Gates, A., and Bennett, C.: *Reversal Tendencies in Reading.* New York, Columbia Univ., 1933.

61. Jones, E.: The child's unconscious. *Papers on Psychoanalysis.* London, Wood, 1923.

62. Kelley, E. C.: *Education for What Is Real.* New York, Harper, 1927.

63. Klein, M.: A contribution to the theory of intellectual inhibition. *Internat. J. Psychoanalysis, XII,* 1931.

64. Klopfer, B., and Kelley, D. M.: *The Rorschach Technique.* New York, World Bk. Co., 1942.

65. Ladd, M. R.: *The relation of social economic and personal characteristics to reading ability.* Teachers College Contributions to Education, No. 582, New York, Columbia Univ. 1933.

66. Levy, S.: Figure drawing as a projective technique, in *Projective Psychology.* L. E. Abt and L. Bellak, Editors. New York, Knopf, 1950.

67. Lindquist, E. F.: *Statistical Analyses in Educational Research.* New York, Houghton, 1940.

68. Liss, E.: Libidinal fixations as pedagogic determinants. *Am. J. Orthopsychiat., 5:*126-131, 1935.

69. Machover, K.: *Personality Projection in the Drawing of the Human Figure.* Springfield, Illinois, Charles C. Thomas, 1949.

70. Mahler, M. S.: Pseudo-imbecility. *Psychoanalyt. Quart., 11:*149, 1942.

71. McCready, E. B.: Defects in the zone of language (Word-deafness and word-blindness) and their influence in education and behavior. *Am. J. Psychiat., 6:*267-277, 1926.

72. McGann, M.: Dramatic dialogues for simultaneous treatment of reading and personality problems. *J. Educational Psychol., 38:*97, 1947.

73. McKee, P.: *Reading and Literature in the Elementary School.* New York, Houghton, 1934.

74. Meek, L.: *A Study of Learning and Retention in Young Children.* New York, Columbia Univ., 1925.

75. Miale, F. R., and Harrower, M. R.: Personality structure

in the psychoneuroses. *Rorschach Research Exchange,* *8*:46-70, 1944.

76. Monroe, M.: Thirty-Fourth Yearbook, National Society for the Study of Education. *Educational Diagnosis,* pp. 214-215.

77. Moses, L. E.: Non parametric statistics for psychological research. *Psychological Bull., 2:*122-143, 1952.

78. Munroe, R. L.: *Prediction of the Adjustment and Academic Performance of College Students by a Modification of the Rorschach Method.* Stanford Univ. Press, Applied Psychology Monograph, *7:*104, 1945.

79. Murphy, L. B., and Ladd, H.: *Emotional Factors in Learning.* New York, Columbia Univ. Press, 1944.

80. National Society for the Study of Education, The forty-eighth yearbook, Part II, *Reading in the Elementary School.* Chicago, Univ. Chicago Press, 1949.

81. Neubauer, P. B.: Basic considerations in the application of therapy and education to parent groups. *Internat. J. Group Psychotherapy, III:*3 315-319, July, 1953.

82. Newell, N.: For non-readers in distress. *Elementary School J., 32:*183-195, 1931.

83. Olson, W. C.: *Problem Tendencies in Children.* Minneapolis, Univ. Minnesota Press, 1930.

84. Orton, S. T.: Word-blindness in school children. *Arch. Neurol. & Psychiat.,* London, 14, 1925.

85. Orton, S. T.: *Reading, Writing and Speech Problems in Children.* Norton, New York, 1937.

86. Pearson, G. H. J.: A survey of learning difficulties in children. pp. 332-386. *Psychoanalyt. Study Child,* vol. VII. New York, Internat. Univ. Press, 1952. pp. 448.

87. Peck, H. B.: *Together We Live.* A manual for the study of group therapy. Unpublished manuscript.

88. Peck, H. B., and Bellsmith, V.: *Treatment of the Delinquent Adolescent.* New York, Family Service Association of America, 1954.

89. Percival, W. P.: *A Study of the Courses and Subjects of School Failure.* Doctors dissertation, New York, Columbia

Univ., 1926.

90. Powdermaker, F.: Psychoanalytic concepts in group therapy. *Internat. J. Group Therapy, 1,* 1951.

91. Powdermaker, F. B., and Frank, J. D.: *Group Psychotherapy,* Cambridge, Massachusetts, Harvard, 1953.

92. Preston, M. I.: The reaction of parents to reading failures. *Child Development, 19:*173, 1939.

93. Rabin, A.: A short form of the Wechsler Bellevue Test. *J. Appl. Psychol., 27:*320-324, 1943.

94. Rapaport, D.: *Diagnostic Psychological Testing, II,* Chicago, Yr. Bk. Pub., 1946.

95. Redl, F.: Resistance in therapy groups. *Human Relations, 3:*307-313, 1948.

96. Redl, F., and Wineman, D.: *Children Who Hate.* Glencoe, Illinois, Free Press, 1951.

97. Redl, F., and Wineman, D.: *Controls from Within,* Glencoe, Illinois, Free Press, 1952.

98. Redmont, R. C.: Description and evaluation of a corrective program for reading disabilities. *J. Educational Psychol., 39:*347-358, 1948.

99. Robinson, H. M.: *Why Pupils Fail in Reading.* Chicago, Univ. Chicago Press, 1946.

100. Rogers, C. R.: *Counseling and Psychotherapy.* New York, Houghton, 1942.

101. Rogers, C. R.: *Client Centered Therapy.* New York, Houghton, 1951.

102. Roman, M., Margolin J., and Harari, C.: Reading disability in the delinquent child. *Presented at American Orthopsychiatric Conference,* 1954. Pending publication.

103. Rorschach, H.: *Psychodiagnostics.* Switzerland, Hans Huber, 1942.

104. Russel, D. H.: Reading and child development. National Society for the Study of Education, the Forty-Eighth Yearbook, Part II, *Reading in the Elementary School,* P. 27.

105. Sargent, H.: Projective methods: Their origins, theory and application in personality research. *Psychological*

Bull., *42*:257-293, 1945.

106. Schafer, R.: *The Clinical Application of Psychological Tests.* New York, Internat. Univ. Press, 1948.

107. Schonell, F. J.: *Backwardness in the Basic Subjects.* Edinburgh, Oliver & Boyd, Ltd., 1942.

108. Schulman, I.: The dynamics of certain reactions of delinquents to group therapy. *Internat. J. Group Therapy, II*:4, 34-43, Oct. 1952.

109. Seashore, H., Wesman, A., and Doppelt, J.: The standardization of the Wechsler Intelligence Scale for Children. *J. Consulting Psychology, 2*:99-110, 1950.

110. Seavey, V.: *Third Mental Measurements Yearbook,* ed. by O. K. Benos. New Brunswick, Rutgers Univ. Press, 1949.

111. Siegal, M.: *The Personality Structure of Children with Reading Disabilities as Compared with Children Presenting Other Clinical Problems.* Doctoral Dissertation, New York, N. Y. Univ., 1951.

112. Skinner, C. E., editor: *Educational Psychology.* New York, Prentice-Hall, 1945.

113. Slavson, S. R.: Differential dynamics of activity and interview group therapy. *Am. J. Orthopsychiat., 17*:293-302, April, 1947.

114. Slavson, S. R., editor: *The Practice of Group Therapy.* New York, Internat. Univ. Press, 1947.

115. Slavson, S. R.: *Analytic Group Psychotherapy,* New York, Columbia Univ. Press, 1950.

116. Smith, K. U.: The role of the commissural systems of the cerebral cortex in the determination of handedness, eyedness and footedness in man. *J. Gen. Psychol., 32*, 1945.

117. Smith, N. B.: *American Reading Instruction.* New York, Silver Burdett & Co., 1934.

118. Spache, G.: *Third Mental Measurements Yearbook,* edited by O. K. Benos. New Brunswick, Rutgers Univ. Press, 1949.

119. Springer, N. N.: A short form of the Wechsler Intelligence Scale as applied to Naval Personnel. *Am. J. Ortho-*

psychiat., *16*:341-344, 1946.

120. Strachey, J.: Some unconscious factors in reading. *The Internat. J. Psycho-analysis*, *XI*:322-331, 1930.

121. Sylvester, E., and Kunst, M. S.: Psychodynamic aspects of the reading problem. *Am. J. Orthopsychiat.*, *13*:69-76, 1943.

122. Traxler, A. E.: *Ten Years of Research in Reading Summary and Bibliography*. Records Bulletin. 32. New York, Ed. Records Bureau, 1941.

123. Tulchin, S. H.: Emotional factors in reading disabilities in school children. *J. Educational Psychol.*, 443-453, 1935.

124. Vorhaus, P. G.: Non reading as an expression of resistance. *Rorschach Research Exchange*, *10*:60-69, 1946.

125. Wechsler, D.: *The Measurement of Adult Intelligence*. Third Edition, Baltimore, Williams & Wilkins, 1944.

126. Wechsler, D.: *Wechsler Intelligence Scale for Children*, Manual. New York, Psychological Corporation, 1949.

127. Weiskopf, E. A.: Intelligent malfunctioning and personality. *J. Abnorm. & Social Psychol.*, *3*:410-423, 1951.

128. White, R. W.: Interpretation of imaginative productions. *Personality and the Behavior Disorders*, Vol. I, edited by J. McV. Hunt. New York, Ronald, 1944.

129. Wilking, S. V.: Personality maladjustment as a causative factor in reading disability. *Elementary School J.*, *42*:268-279, 1941.

130. Wilcoxon, F.: Individual comparisons by ranking methods. *Biometrics Bull.*, *1*:80-82, 1945.

131. Witty, Paul: *Helping Children Read Better*, Chicago, S. R. A., 1950.

132. Witty, P. A., and Kopel, D.: *Reading and the Educative Process*, Boston, Ginn, 1939.

133. Zirbes, L.: Some character and personality problems of remedial cases in reading. *Childhood Education*, *5*:171-176, 1928.

134. *Summary of Proceedings Conference on Control of Juvenile Delinquency*. Washington, D. C., United States Children's Bureau, 1952.